811.54 Op5n
Oppenheimer, Joel.
Names & local habitations

Jargon 59

NAMES & LOCAL HABITATIONS

(Selected Earlier Poems 1951—1972)

DODO

Joel Oppenheimer

NAMES & LOCAL HABITATIONS
(Selected Earlier Poems 1951–1972)

Accolade by Hayden Carruth
Introduction by William Corbett

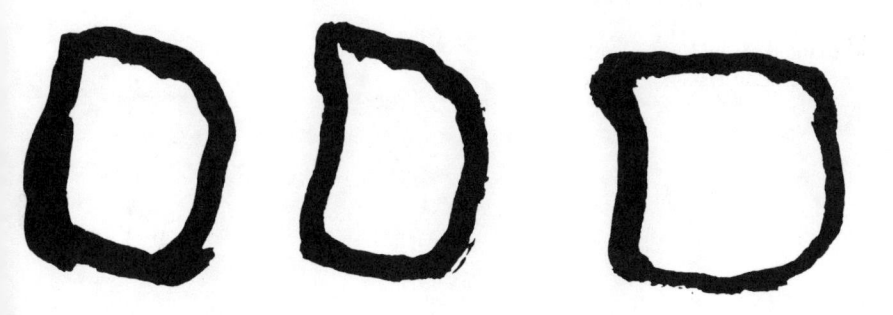

THE JARGON SOCIETY 1988

The poems in NAMES & LOCAL HABITATIONS were originally collected in the following books, whose publishers Joel Oppenheimer wishes to acknowledge:

THE DANCER The Jargon Society (1951)
THE DUTIFUL SON The Jargon Society (1956)
THE LOVE BIT Totem/Corinth Publishers (1962)
JUST FRIENDS/FRIENDS AND LOVERS (POEMS 1959–1962)
The Jargon Society (1980)
IN TIME (POEMS 1962–1968) The Bobbs-Merrill Company (1969)
THE WRONG SEASON The Bobbs Merrill Company (1973)
ON OCCASION (POEMS 1969–1972)
The Bobbs-Merrill Company (1973)

NAMES & LOCAL HABITATIONS. Copyright © 1988 by Joel Oppenheimer. Drawings. Copyright © 1988 by the Estate of Philip Guston. All rights reserved. For information address the publisher:

The Jargon Society, Inc.
Second Floor
411 North Cherry Street
Winston-Salem, North Carolina 27101
(919) 724-7619

Library of Congress Card Catalog Number: 88-81843
ISBN (cloth): 0-912330-66-x

The publication of this book was made possible in part by a grant from the National Endowment for the Arts.

Designed by Thomas Meyer and Jonathan Williams
Typesetting by Graphic Composition, Inc. (Athens, Georgia)
Printed in the United States of America by
Thomson-Shore, Inc. (Dexter, Michigan)

Distributed to the trade by Inland Book Company
254 Bradley Street, East Haven, Connecticut 06512.

this book is for
Jonathan Williams
my first publisher
and still the best

CONTENTS

ACCOLADE, Hayden Carruth   *ix*
INTRODUCTION, William Corbett   *xi*

from **THE DANCER** (1951)   *3*
from **THE DUTIFUL SON** (1956)   *7*
from **THE LOVE BIT** (1962)   *23*
from **JUST FRIENDS/FRIENDS AND LOVERS** (1980)   *45*
    FRIENDS   *49*
    LOVERS   *75*
from **IN TIME** (1969)   *91*
    LOVE   *95*
    US   *129*
from **THE WRONG SEASON** (1973)   *197*
from **ON OCCASION** (1973)   *205*
    OCCASIONS   *209*
    OTHERS   *239*

AUTHOR'S NOTE   *278*
AN INDEX TO TITLES AND FIRST LINES   *279*

ACCOLADE

During the rather long time when I made my living as a free-lance hack I reviewed thousands of books for newspapers and magazines of all kinds. I never turned down an assignment; I couldn't afford to. The great preponderance of these books was mainstream poetry and fiction in the fashion of the day. Some were done well, most were not, which is what one would expect. But almost all were borne down by the weight of pretension and imitativeness into a muck of tedium that clung to my mind. I felt soiled by them. I was.

Then along came a book of poems by Joel Oppenheimer. Such freshness of topic, such originality of perception! These poems were *interesting*—what a relief! And the language was clean and clear and delicately poised—well, not too delicately. Beyond that Oppenheimer was a humorist, he was funny, he was even—rarest of qualities—good-natured, he loved people and places, his poems were celebrations, not at all ritualistic, but spontaneous and genuine. Oppenheimer loved sex, loved food, loved life, loved.

My man, I said. Thereafter I looked for his books, the older ones in second-hand shops, the new ones as they came along. I was never disappointed. And years later when I finally met Oppenheimer I discovered exactly the man I had imagined from reading his poems.

Now his earlier work has been collected in one book, and the occasion is for all of us to celebrate, including perhaps especially young readers who haven't known the work before. Here is a poetic life in America during our most troubled decades; naturally some of the poems are angry. But the joyful ones prevail, I think, and that's a blessing, and I hope many, many people will enjoy them and benefit from them. This is the kind of book that makes me want to run out in the street and shout, "Viva! Viva Oppenheimer!"—and believe me from an old-time reviewer you couldn't get a better recommendation. At any rate that's how I intend it.

Hayden Carruth

INTRODUCTION

Essential Use

This book opens with a poem Joel Oppenheimer wrote at Black Mountain College. He spent three years there and was, of course, a student of Charles Olson's. Since Donald Allen's anthology *The New American Poetry* placed the Black Mountain School on the map of American poetry no poet who attended has been allowed to graduate. Some labels won't go away. They may be followed by "but his work is . . ." yet remain as a matter of convenience, what Hugh Kenner calls "a classroom inaccuracy." Joel Oppenheimer's understandable desire to have his poems speak for themselves has led him, in at least one biographical note, to omit BMC altogether. To introduce more than twenty years of his work let me paraphrase A.J. Muste's reply to his draft board when baited with a question imagining Hitler's attentions toward his sister and "delicately interpose" a few words between these nearly three hundred pages of poetry and the category Joel Oppenheimer has been lumped into.

A former student of Olson's at Buffalo once described class with the man as a rocket ship ride. When you blasted off you had no idea of your destination, but the trip left you exhilarated as you never imagined you could be in a classroom. You might not grasp all that Olson said, but you were inspired by the charge of his mind and talk. Olson's intellectual dominance through volumes of talk was matched by his 6'8" physical dominance. An overwhelming, unforgettable presence. But, and this is crucial, poets and writers who studied with him were, on the evidence of their work, more influenced by the spirit of his teaching than the letter of his writing. Oppenheimer gives him this credit:

> "i have to speak in different images
> but you told me a long time ago
> to speak in my own, and I believed
> that."

The title of this introduction taken from Olson's essay "Projective Verse" sums up this spirit. The doctrine of use is Joel Oppenheimer's true Black Mountain heritage. The rest is all pigeon hole, sloppy and inaccurate. As Oppenheimer writes in a recent essay, "Black Mountain was, indeed, the first place I'd ever been or lived where poetry had a function . . ." The vivifying heart of Oppenheimer's endeavor has been to extend this function, to make poems of essential use for the world at large.

At the moment American poetry, in school and out, is more a matter of difficulty than, say, the pleasurable exercise of the imagination. The use it is put to by a great many teachers is to teach the hard work of close reading, analysis and paraphrase. Students are convinced that poetry is beyond their experience and imagination. The demand is to discover and understand what the poet means. On the way to this they are often shown their ignorance. Ignorance that can feel like unworthiness before great works of literature whose value centuries and generations declare. Who needs this humiliation in the name of a lofty good the culture chiefly endorses as only fit for training the young? No wonder the majority emerge from this "rigor" never again to read a poem.

One of the many bizarre consequences of this hickory stick approach is that poetry such as Oppenheimer's, poetry written in the common tongue be it written by Kenneth Rexroth or Paul Goodman, both of whom are kin to Oppenheimer, is rarely looked at in school. As poetry is pushed further toward the margins of society fewer are able, and these are mostly poets, to persist in believing that poetry is more a condition of what you are capable of imagining than what you know. Since imagination is served last, or served not at all, it trembles, fearful of getting the poem "wrong."

Knowledge is not the enemy nor is history. The enemy is he who makes the poem depend on what you know, on the history of literature recent or distant, *before* it depends on the reader's imagination. The enemy presents poetry as a test to which only the initiate has the answers. Even the genuinely difficult work of an Olson or Robert Duncan is disfigured by this approach because their poetry becomes proof that poetry must be explained. The more intimidating the poem the more intimidating the swarm of criticism that surrounds it. Evelyn Waugh remembered his friends chanting T.S. Eliot's "Lady, three white leopards sat under a juniper tree" just for the joy of it. The words captivated them. Today poetry is explained before it can captivate. You endure this, fill up your blue book and sell the text for cash.

Joel Oppenheimer doesn't ride this hobby horse in his poems. I have been on it to suggest why his work has received so little critical attention. If Black Mountain is one strike then the clarity of his poems, their manly directness are strikes two and three. Strange but true. If a poem is what must be explained the poet who addresses the reader head on because he wants him to get what he is saying has committed a vulgar gesture and made rude noises forcing intimacy. Frank O'Hara wanted his poems to exist "Lucky Pierre style" between poet and reader. This becomes a foursome and the game might as well be bridge when the explainer or poet-explainer chaperones the poem. Basta! That this is so may trouble Oppenheimer, but he has had the nerve to ignore it. He has been too busy making poems of use to complain in his poems about the tough row they have to hoe. His poems have the indifference of the truly sincere. They are here for us to make of them what use we can.

What they strive to be was set out by Oppenheimer in a statement he gave *The New American Poetry:*

> "i see william carlos williams as my poetic grandfather, take occasional verse as 'the highest form of poetry', believe a poem is an answer to a question you didn't know you'd asked yourself, and tend to write a discursive juxtapositional and highly personal body of work."

Oppenheimer found little to excite him when he read the Randall Jarrell selected Williams at twenty. But he persisted, and when he came "to the two versions of the locust tree poem" he heard not only what Williams was about but must have glimpsed his own future. The skinny plunge of "The Locust Tree in Flower"

>   Among
>   of
>   green
>
>   stiff
>   old
>   bright

remains as a kind of spine in Oppenheimer's work. His poems have an equivalent lean, virile and vertical rush down the page. They move not with the passionate, impatient jolts and leaps common to Williams but with a steady propulsion. Oppenheimer does not pause for the conventionally beautiful line or fine phrase. His free verse is broken so that a line seldom stands alone as a quotable complete thought. The parts of his poems rarely draw attention from the whole. There is a narrative persistence to them, a getting on with it, even though the voice is emphatically lyric.

Voice, in the sense of being true to one's native accents, is what Oppenheimer found in Williams most suited to his own use. You will hear and feel the voice in these poems as an actual speaking voice. Oppenheimer is a garrulous poet, "Garrulous to the last" as Walt Whitman described himself, who tapped early into his voice and has stayed with it. But he's not writing to hear himself talk. His is a listener's voice. The poems are tuned by his inner ear as he manipulates and heightens for effect the accents he has picked up.

If Oppenheimer is not a poet for whom technical matters are of primary interest he is, to use an image from his beloved baseball, the sort of infielder who fields cleanly every ball he gets to. It's a matter of positioning. Over the years, to continue it, he has learned to play the hitters, to vary the length of his line, to keep his poems supple and responsive, in shape for his requirements. He has not sought to improve on Williams's prosody but adapted it to his own peculiar needs and desires. This means you'll have a general recognition, you'll have heard this voice before, but it won't be until as you read on, that the tang that is Oppenheimer's alone will rise in your ear.

As an occasional poet, and I think Oppenheimer's verse sticks to the statement he gave in 1960, there are occasions that appear to have had no charm for him. He has steered clear of those that turn on so many Academic poets. There are no poems in this book inspired by European landmarks (has he ever been?), or dedicated to certified great works of art, nor to agonies of self as revealed in some memory Madeleine. Oppenheimer is infrequently a poet of memory and just as infrequently a poet of events that, if you can hear the voice of Walter Cronkite, "alter and illuminate our time." His focus is local. You believe that he knows first hand the here and now he's talking about. He is a poet of experience who, the poems convince me, does not so much rise to an occasion but make his poems an occasion that might otherwise have gone unobserved.

Oppenheimer writes often and well of what it means to be a man in love with women and loved by them. He does not shy away from his own failures nor the awkwardness of his conduct. Sex in his poems is often low comedy, a comedy of lust, fleshy encounters and unexpected, not always pleasant, revelations. These have a dailiness, the pith and grit of life unresolved but not unredeemed by poetry—frustrating, sometimes hilarious and engrossing. And he writes in sweet, sad and angry tones of what it has meant to be a son and father. If there is still a positive sense that can be claimed for the adjective masculine then I claim it for this poet. There are poems that celebrate birthdays, weddings and the newly dead and again the stance is local, the voice familiar. Oppenheimer doesn't so much make something of the occasion as he makes the poem the occasion. I am repeating myself, but bear with me as I think the distinction I'm groping toward is a revealing one.

Let me compare Oppenheimer's work to that of Auden and Brecht. In Auden's occasional poems I hear an authoritative public voice, a voice that tells me it is not only speaking to me but for me. It is a literary voice robust, confident and high toned. It is the voice we are taught to accept as great. Brecht is grubby. His is a raw and vulgar voice that you want to, and feel perfectly capable of, talking back to. It's hit or miss, spur of the moment and unmindful of its manners. No value judgment is implied here. In poetry the poet chooses to be patrician or a man in the street, and either way he may use an occasion, be it marriage or death, as a pretext. To me one seems more to lecture (Auden) than engage (Brecht), but this is merely an aspect of their differing natures. If Oppenheimer made a conscious choice it is not to "mischoose/ the target and then aim/ too well." He is not the American Brecht, but his poems have a similar colloquial directness and thinking out loud immediacy.

In his poem to Marilyn Monroe, about whom he also wrote a book, Oppenheimer announced, "i am a/ sports-loving jewish/ intellectual/ writer". To this could be added, "a working American/ citizen of New York City/ who became a teacher." His is an individual's voice affirming, in the American tradition, the authority of the individual man or woman who has been there. His poetry is autobiographical in the American tradition that encompasses Emily Dickinson and Ezra Pound, Elizabeth Bishop and Allen Ginsberg. Oppenheimer writes more to record than confess, and in keeping with this his autobiography is as much a matter of tone as it is of subject.

What this adds up to is a poet who refreshes the words we use everyday through his careful attention to them and accuracy in making poems we can grasp "at least," he has recently written, "at some simple level, no matter how far it goes beyond that level." The refreshment he brings is one use we can make of his poetry; words clarified by his use made available to us for our own. Because Oppenheimer means us to grasp what he has grasped, however tentatively, from his own experience we cannot help but think of our own lives, our own lovers and friends and family and the world through which we daily move. Oppenheimer's poems are a sort of compass that allows the reader to locate himself, to have a keener sense of where he is. It is a poetry that assumes by its reliance on a man's individual voice that we all have voices, and if we can hear his we can better attend to the voice with which we read, to the particulars of our own experience as these are called to attention. Like Whitman Oppenheimer's poems make a path for us. We look to the grass under our boot soles to see where another has gone and to contemplate our own going. It's not the examined life so much as life lived with a respect for all its complexity, for the many twists and turns it takes right under our noses.

So, you are about to read a big book of poems by a poet who wholeheartedly desires that he reach you, that what he has sunk his teeth into and chewed to the bone be communicated in order that, and I think *this* is Oppenheimer's essential use, significant experiences occurring in the ordinary run of things may be intensified through order and made memorable. This will result in pleasure and some necessary pains. The literal experiences do not produce these sensations. These are reached, to give the last words to Oppenheimer's spiritual grandfather William Carlos Williams, through what the poet makes "with such intensity of purpose that it lives with an intrinsic movement of its own to verify its authenticity."

William Corbett

NAMES & LOCAL HABITATIONS

(Selected Earlier Poems 1951–1972)

from **THE DANCER** (1951)

THE DANCER

for Katherine Litz

for Katy
        stands rooted, herself
to one spot
        becomes:

                the only spot we know.

Grows, in this spot, among:
                flowers
                love
                whatever's
her particular
        as we too
have particulars
        but she
flies free
    pulling.

Delight, unvarying
        Katy dances;
her dance's conjure:
        flowers;
her legs are suns to light
the seeds around, while
            on the wooden floor
her feet
know mud, know snow, know
spring

from **THE DUTIFUL SON** (1957)

AN ANSWER

what mercy is not
strained, what justice
not bought, what
love not used come thru.
my lady asks me
not without reason
where is pleasure in it. where sense.
my ear is not worth much
in these matters, tho it be
shelllike, and acute.
offer beyond a dedication?
and a particular care.

THE LOVER

every time
the same way
wondering when
this when that.
if you were a
plum tree. if you
were a peach
tree.

THE BUS TRIP

    images of J——— assail him.
the moon used to, but the moon is
an illuminated clock, he feels.
it does not particularly remind him or instruct.
when he rides on the bus with
drawings, a bag of apples, his
wife and lovely child, is he any
less or more the, a, fool.
if his child were not beautiful
what could he do and live. if his wife
were not beautiful what could he do and live.
these things are insanely important
to him. tho he lose his power facing them.
a woman, girl, across from him is
more beautiful than the world. he is
repelled. and pulls back. death.
the death of beauty, when it is beautiful, he
finds her. and dead. across from him
in a bus. the old man beside her. they
talk in italian.   a heavy sigh escapes him
when he goes. away from that across from him.
descends into the street. sketches, apples,
child, helps his pregnant wife. she
smiles. the child runs down
the street. images of J———
assail him. constantly. what shall he do.

THE TIDE

she sits
braiding
her hair at
the sea's
edge—and
the tide
is coming
in! and
she sits in the
fringe of the
waves, braiding
her
hair, and
the tide—and
dark hair—and in
the greenblue water coming
in, seaweed
afloat—greenblue,
and for once, wet
dark with the water
her dress is not
purple, but
no color at
all—her
hands, braiding
her
hair

THE BATH

he will insist on
reading things into her simplest act.
her bath, which she takes
because he wills it so. her bath
she takes to cleanse herself.
ritual. ritual always
in his life. she takes her bath
to ready herself.
and himself more often than not decides
she wants him unbathed. manlike.
what he is most pleased about is
her continuing bathing.
in his tub. in his water. wife.

THE GOD

where
he went
violets
grew
behind
him
she
followed
after
picking
them
and decorated
herself

LOVESONG

in time, in time they
will say it all i mean images of
death and the act of
loving.
a flaring pomegranate has
more seeds than one man can
possibly spit
out, the juice runs down
from the same corners of
the chin where the
beard refuses to grow.

THE SLIDING POND SONNET

first she come down it ta dum ta dum ta
straight then she ta ta ta dum ta dum ta
hung by her heels on fi de fi de de
her back come down and stopped fi de fi de
by braking against the ta ta dum ta
sides. went up and come ta dum ta dum ta
down on her belly went fi de fi de
under the ladder fi fi de fi de
swung up her feet climbing ta dum ta dum
inside the ladder right dum ta ta dum
in my boy's face him struggling fi de fi
his own way up the outside. fi fi fi
her first name fiona age ta dum de
8 honey blond and discreet. fi de de

PROVENCE

today i bathed my feet, like
some irish maiden hoping
for a lover
        —she would have to be
long-haired; i trust only long-haired women

and it is summer here, and still
men are talking about
another land, which had been
impossibly green and fruitful

yet i might have done
better, there, myself. i

might have written good songs, if
she had been faithful, and better, if
she were not, and also, polemic
against the betrayer, political,
tearing him down; with a choice
of rhetoric—between
rapier and the two-bitted
woods-axe, which i seem to favor,
being the man i am, using it
file-sharpened, to a good edge

well, as it is, either
silence, or silence and
action either way most brutal is
expected; and i would prefer a
milieu demanding hard work
—and fitting words to a tune

'fair night,
 early rising,
 the sun up,
 the mist still rising. and
 in the woods, sounds of small animals

        it is a hard travelling, toward you, with
        a hidden road

        it is hard to tell what
        i am complaining about

        wanting to know, i guess,
        that it is not even this for you

        which, whether or not it is a fine thing to be
        saying, especially at this point, still

'remember this hand
 which touched you

'be ready upon the white palfrey, the
 small and strong one, with
 spirit; three
 days from now,
 at dawn.'

AN APPROACH TO LE BAIN

the incredible delicacy

with which you
conquer yourself

Ma domna the bath you take

it's an act of giving
of presenting yourself, yourself
presenting yourself

Ma domna the bath you take

it's an infinite tenderness
with which you respect or
bow yourself before

incredible incredible Ma domna

as in the arch of the back or
leg bent to the
cloth one feels
you have tied yourself
so completely have you put
yourself before it

Ma domna the bath you take

THE ANSWER

this is
the morning.
for us in this
portion love
has no solid
grip.
your
baby is
crying. it
is a new
day.

THE COUPLE

if i don't bring you
flowers. if i don't have any
flowers. delicate grubby violets.
chrysanthemums for your coat.
only children. what has that got
to do with it.

any child is isaac.
brushwood and sticks.
the burning bush in the hill's side.
jesus strung from a dogwood.

it is not fair
where is fairness. if she is not
fair where is fairness. if flowers.
apples. peaches and pears
for the summer. an edible potato.

the stain of the dogwood
is in you. what now.
mushrooms. or underground
truffles. a pig with a ring
in his snout. he is hungry.
the stain of the dogwood.

who cries for another's
pain hasn't enough of his own.
where are my children they
leave me here knocking wood.

what is there i haven't invented
contrived cut out of the
whole cloth. some day to
make it easier, with more
pleasure. that is a pleasure.

how else to be fecund if not
to put up with a man.

THE PEACHES

when your belly
is swoln. when your
belly is full. when there is a child.
never in this situation
words like peaches.
to bite into. savor.
peel the skin
with your teeth.
bit of a peach. sweet.
flavor. filling myself
on your extension.
i will talk to you about this.
let us eat a peach after supper.

THE GARDENER

on the left branch, a
blossom. on the
top branch, a blossom.
which child is this.
which flowering
of me. which
gold white bloom.
which the force of my life.

A

the eye, the
eye, i see
my son

the eye, the
eye, my
son sees me

he is taking
five steps towards
his mother, she
is holding
two hands out to
meet him

the eye, the eye,
i see my wife

acutely, in a similar
way, she
sees me, the
eye, the eye, the
eye

she is holding out
two hands to
meet him

THE FEEDING

when she fed the
child, he fought back,
what does
he know of fruitfulness.
after she yelled at him
he was contrite.
but not even fearing she
meant it. a common decency you might say.
and again, then, spilled his milk.
and then looked up. smiling at her,
pleasantly, and, damn it, without
malice, even.

MAY DAY IN THE PARK

the word peace
is obliterated
a more fierce indictment
was scrawled on washington's
leg, above
the knee

rosa

rosa eats it

from **THE LOVE BIT** (1962)

PREFACE

geometry's my
ax, sd

    euclid, i
cut everybody.

BLUE FUNK

i wish all the
mandragora grew
wild, screaming.

and in the cattails,
pussywillows, etc.,
wind soft as
eastern standard time.

wind soft as the
last time you
did it. wind soft
as a soft wind.

i wish we
bathed in essence of
ginseng, for our health.

i wish eastern standard
time, etc., rang the
changes in our hearts.

A POSTCARD

let's put it this
way, if you had a
bullet, why don't
you write

your friends yr cousins
with the blunted soft
lead end jack london
said the
      'best to use'
and no erasure
necessary. that is

i wldn't know whether
to put it thru my
head, or bite it?

what about it, i sd.
what about all of us
standing here with
the knife in our
backs.
    cha
    cha cha cha.

    only
    a
    rose!

    cha cha.

biting it, old
friend. and the
family?

A HEART FULL OF

a heart full of
garbage. that was
the novel she wanted
to write, rich and
beguiling in its angers.
i wonder how she
does it, forces her
way thru into something
comprehensible, makes of her
children presentable items
of her own agenda, supplies
her husband with affection
even in the middle of a
night when he has failed her,
refuses to remember as if
to deny it happened.
yet on his head spins that
light touch, and his chin
which her hand caressed
sprouts beardedly with
love. this is not a novel
but a way and light.

FORMAL VERSE, FATHER OF SEVENTY-THREE

what i worry about is you and what
you worry about is him and what he
worries about is a bottle of beer
which worries about me because i'm

how's that for a quatrain huh bayby
how's that for a quatrain

what myself hooked up with was
two arms just sitting there looking
out at me saying come on old friend

that's why some of this worrying

i mean when i say like social i.e.
whose problem is it to be old friend
seeing as who is it was who put it up now

how's that for a theory huh bayby
how's that for a theory

what i worry about is me and what
i worry about is certainly me and what i
worry about is me and not at all at all
of problems which happen today

MID-PASSAGE

as if i were going to make
myself over, or, starting
from scratch, cultivate
me, i got some new
glasses, a haircut, allowed
the barber to trim up my beard.

soon, i'll have a new cap, and
maybe a derby, i'll buy me new
slacks, shoes, two or three pairs.
i'll do myself up, and the
poem will emerge fresh, shining
as a tulip on easter morning, my
friends will invite me to dinner,
my wife'll curl languorously in
bed. like a tulip easter morning.

THE ANYBODY BLUES

This poem is for Roger Touhy

well he cries out behind bars
his own interpretaysh well he cries out.
put it in the lines between man
put it in the lines between.

and careless too; man nobody listens.
man nobody ever listens.
nobody ever listens.
but an f.b.i. man listens, always.
always. ain't that the way man.

MARE NOSTRUM

a bosom of
green buds,
ass like a
valentine.

the spring
rolls around,
moiling me
up.

(also green buds on
hedges, my heart
in every dogwood
blossom, even tulip,
even pink daisies)

i'm forced to it again.
                            old
lady with a
bosom of green buds, also
an ass like a valentine, etc.

THE CHART

the anchorage for explosives is in his heart;
his balls are a restricted area.
he feels no advantage, has nothing to peg onto.
if he sheds his skin his bones will rise.
but even the valley of bones is measured,
ezekiel cries, forty nine miles long and
forty nine miles wide. his dry bones.

CARTOGRAPHY

the ceiling of his bedroom
cracks into map shapes.
an island. harbors sunk in the island's perimeter.
two great rivers. a lake at the confluence.
while on the phone he draws plans of houses abstractedly,
or replots the defense of gettysburg.
on the bedroom wall, in detail, san francisco bay,
the hills marked and notated with the addresses of friends.
on the walls of the john,
hand-drawn and accurately scaled,
the devil's den and the round tops.
the lines outside vicksburg, petersburg, the wilderness
mile by mile engraved in his mind. carried with him
white oaks, where his great-grandfather fell.
he does not even know if this fact, this death,
exists for him outside of white oaks.
shall he not die also when he has no direction
before him, no plan of action, no campaign.
does he not find it impossible to move without
at least compass, or sun, gunter's chain, or a
measured pace, or the regular plat of a city's streets.
at one time his pace was exactly three feet.
with it he could determine miles, within a few yards.
or put it this way. if in his own islands
he could move freely. if he could take himself and his worlds.
build a continent of them. that might break him free.
if his children were more than milestones to him.
or if his wife more than the tracings of his finger
outlined before him. that might break him free.
but he will find it necessary to move himself.
this is the first action.

ON PARADE

in the neck the
strain of carrying
himself
      the knobbly
legs something
must bite to
move them on so

           lips
gently nibble at them
under green tender leaves splayed
from the lower branches

no man able to
handle the monstrous, no
man able to assess
this particular value, the

giraffe eating, knocking
down telegraph wires doing
forty miles of grassy
plain an
      hour.

the giraffe
does move.

FOR THE BARBERS

tenderly as a
barber trimming
it off i
sing my songs, like
a barber stropping
a razor, i rage.

tho the song be
pure as anything, if
the mode be not right,
if the mode
        be not pure

the calculation of
a barber is immeasurable,
the cunning, the sly
skittering about the
head
    if a needle were
dug in the middle of
the cranium would it
do more damage?

            oh the
professionals what we
should fear.

TRIPLETS

thus
for
the warm
and loving
heart
the
inmost
and
most
private
part
shall
ever
be
sweet
eros'
dart.

thus for the warm and loving heart
the inmost and most private part
shall ever be sweet eros' dart.

thus for the warm
and loving heart the
inmost and most
private part shall ever be
sweet eros' dart.

BLOOD

How, ever else to
do it? But with
love, and a new way
to comb my moustache?

Or she said: you
and your old
man, sitting here both
in your underwear!

APRIL FOOL

birds sing and my
son too, in the
morning.
with words, without
words, in the morning.
singing inside the
house, outside the
house, in the morning.
it's five o'clock in the morning.
she's silk smooth
beside me, doesn't stir;
the older boy stays
sleeping, doesn't stir.
like birds, like
a houseful of birds.
and me the early
worm.

MY BLUE HEAVEN

tho it
could be different, my
bed's like
chile—not
cold, but narrow.
i'm constrained to
sleeping on my
side, and hover
over the edge all night.

every time
after i
haven't made it in
a while . . .
feeling i may
have goofed it,
tho i wonder more
and more what it's all
about.

we are all guilty of that
indiscretion, eating
daisies left and
right, when there's
almost anything else
available, always.

THE SCENE

half-bent and crouched holding
to the iron fence
grotesque, distorted by the evening light

with her cries to keep him off
what more could he do, but
reach vaguely out and touch.

what more she, but cry,
continue crying, holding to the fence,
in the crazy evening light.

AN UNDEFINED TENDERNESS

an undefined tenderness came
into the relationship. we were
afraid of such things, still, it
became necessary, and we learned
not to put it down—or put it
this way, time and a senseless
friction wore a smooth edge.
finally, i think, we could face to it:
there is no love possible beyond
those first moments of fire and
trembling passion. this makes more
sense than a roomful of roses,
your ass, and my heart. and, desire
burns fiercely in me yet, i
ought to be satisfied.

LEAVE IT TO ME BLUES

from the heart of a flower
a stalk emerges; in each fruit
there are seeds. we turn our
backs on each other so often,
we destroy any community of
interest. yet our hearts are
seeded with love and care sticks
out of our ears. but there is no
bridge unless it is the wind which
whistles our bare house, tearing
the slipcovers apart and constantly
removing the tablecloth covering
it (the table) like a shroud (the
shroud of what the table could mean,
if only we were hungry enough to
care), and we cut ourselves off
because we discovered each man is
an island, detached. man, the
mainland is flipped over the moon.
all i have to depend on is effort,
and the moon goes round and round
in the evening sky. my sons will
make it if they ever reach age,
but how to take care i don't know.
it doesn't get better. on the other
hand, even with answers, where
would we be, out in the cold, with
an old torn blanket, and no one
around us to cry.

THE BREADWINNER

a quieter man could not
succeed, one not intent
on repetition.
what else but a renewing instant
our one entry into it
whatever our view or interest.
a renewing entry into whatever
force it is sustains us sustains us.
a renewing entry re-presenting
itself, constantly,
as a pot of pink azaleas
pervades the whole house.

APOCRYPHA

what we dream of in our easiest
moments, to come into like
virgins under the arched canopy
of flowers, bowing ourselves
before the altar, even turning
ourselves inside and out, a
sacramental relationship perhaps,
but i prefer to think we drive
ourselves too wildly toward talk,
to use a common language, as if
it existed. my wife's
eyes closed, then, slowly, each lid
taking precedence slowly to cut off
the vision, and on each strand of
her hair, there appeared, as in frenzy,
a quiet bloody drop, wreathing her head.

THE YOUNG BLOODS

what will happen to your
daughter, friend, your
lovely lovely daughter

as my sons grow fierce,
friend, as my sons
grow more and more fierce

nowhere near bearded they
lust insatiably, friend, nothing
will ever fill them

and myself, this young,
i already make my delight,
friend, perceiving this

THE LOVE BIT

the colors we depend on are
red for raspberry jam, white
of the inside thigh, purple as
in deep, the blue of moods, green
cucumbers (cars), yellow stripes down
the pants, orange suns on ill-omened days, and black as the
dirt in my fingernails.
also, brown, in the night,
appearing at its best when
the eyes turn inward, seeking
seeking, to dig everything but
our own. i.e. we make it crazy or
no, and sometimes in the afternoon.

THE TORN NIGHTGOWN

it seemed to me when i saw her
the white white of a
light in the midst of darkness,
the softness as a belly is, also the
rip, to not forget this rape.
and i wondered then in the night
if all wives had such badges.
and bitterly, if over each
set of stretch marks, over
each veined breast, each brown
nipple, there floated soft and
white a torn nightgown. and thought
of all of us who turn heavily
on our beds at night. of the heart
which ponderously grasps its
way back, great sea creature caught
far up on the beach, a monstrous polyp or
jellyfish. of the lungs painfully
beating in used air to bring us back
sweating to face air. of the nameless
faceless images we dealt with, giving
our all. of the snorts and grunts and
great cracks of wind exhaled fighting
off the wild animals, keeping the beasts
at bay, while we slept. of all the legs
that might be slid between, all the
buttocks held firm and resilient,
all the nipples erected and tweaked
between thumb and first finger.
of all the bodies male and
female to be made love to
beneath the grinding of light,
air, darkness, all the
constituents and elements.
the cat makes it in the alley meanwhile,
the neighbor makes it next door, heaving and
grunting and shaking the springs.

panting in the dark night, lusting
again and again for warmth, for
a semblance of love. when day comes
the cock rises and crows he crows.
but night is the day of my cock.

Philip Guston 1970

from **JUST FRIENDS/FRIENDS AND LOVERS** (1980)

ORPHEUS

therefore to open
mouth, and let
the voice

        flayed, and eaten, piece
        by lean piece, and with what
        savorings, and with what
        shovings of the greasy fingers
        to the mouth, to get
        full flavors

who, also, went
down, and, came
up, a
coming back, and,
then, hid

he fell to the
cannibal girls
after this

FRIENDS

A GRACE FOR PAINTERS

for p. g.

where you are there are chairs, some
you can sit in feeling the fibre of
the chair itself, some there is

a red throw pillow, it might be
uncomfortable, i have been in these
situations, it looks lovely, you
end up moving it vertically to the
side or discarding it altogether,
on some chairs it works.

                      and my father discussing
                      the possible move to an
                      apartment, what do they
                      need a house, just my
                      father, mother, aunt, says
                      i might want his old easy
                      chair, my mother says it
                      breaks your behind, my
                      father says he might like
                      it nevertheless; a wise
                      man, i haven't had an
                      easy chair in ten years now.

and in the sleeper there is a
white streak dimly seen somewhere in the
middle of the painting more to the
bottom than the top, i said there is
hope, and joe: yeah, open it up.
he laughed, the painters, he said,
only see the colors

                however, even the
alchemist is sitting on a chair, he
needs perhaps the steady support in

his search for the secret, perhaps we
all need that chair bob was talking
about, oh no, perhaps we will find out.

a secret semantics of the soul, then,
in which chairs figure as a place you
could sit down, and there is, perhaps,
a hassock in front of each one, for
those with bad legs, the legs go first,
as jiggs with his gout stretches out
his casted leg upon it, the ease is
evident.

      and pillows for your head at
night. god give you grace as the
bottle sits upon the table, or the
cup; as the table stands beside the
chair; as all eight legs descend and
rest, firmly, upon the ground we
deal with; as the paintings sit, themselves
upon the canvas there before us.

i have entered into a world where crimson
becomes an entity i believe in.

OKAY

for c. o.

money is paper i
issue anew for love, or
love is paper money
we run the presses
faster

    paper: i write this on

who else controlling
that credit, where else
to spend it, a bottle
a day keeps . . . and
we may yet hit chinatown
too, to spend spend spend
what we have built up
silently and alone

let it rain down, money
exists, money exists in
the backs of hidden cars,
in paychecks the ends
of weeks

    you are well-come
to this place where i didn't know
what the money was for, where
no one ate food even,
no one got hungry damn it,
nor even let you find out
if you were really thirsty!
if you were really thirsty!

(they tasted good, he said, they
tasted good)

money is non-interest
making love, money is the
credit freely spent, money
is what lines the pockets and
the streets, this is the *apple*, money
all the goddamned place over,
i thought finally some ought
to be spent, give me credit, hah,
for that
         (i won't stop the
puns either, or measure the
jokes accurately

and the worst part is, of
course, pockets lined with
money, take off knowing the
stores are closed, it's after
three and no more beer,
hoping that one place will
sell it, and the damned car has
a flat twelve blocks from no
where, and, money and all, like
a team of pros, we got to
get down and change it, in
the middle of the goddamned
street. money is a variable
measure we carry in our
pants, and it's got numbers
on it; money sometimes is
love paper we issue anew and
anew, let the presses roll,
ride it love, you'll never
get rich that way, thank you

THE BOYS WHOSE FATHERS

for f.k.

pablo neruda was one, so
was franz kline, and so also,
some of my generation;
the boys whose fathers
were railroad men

they, as their mothers,
measured out time by the
sound of an engine or whistle;

and the tracks in chile,
as the tracks in wilkes-barre,
and even the tracks in
mauch chunk (later they
changed the name: jim thorpe
pennsylvania—and he lies
buried there because they would
do this for him, and at each
corner of the grave dirt from
the fields he played on, and
not far off, carlisle

        "where's the team?"
        "it's here. he runs
          the mile and up,
          and *he* does everything
          else."
              the answer a
        coach dreams of, pop
        warner to lafayette's)

and the tracks in matoon too,
and in harmon-on-hudson, they
all have gravel has to be
tamped down, ties replaced,

the rails straightened, on the
horseshoe bend going up from
old fort they work from one end
to the other, constantly straightening,
singing of course an old song, the
chorus sharp, the verse long and languid,
and the clanking of the crowbars as they
set themselves ready to heave.

yes pablo neruda they are all
to be worked on, they all ring
with the shiny engines, the
dusty engines, did you know
not one steam locomotive built
here in this country since the war,
no more anything but the diesels?

but i am lying pablo neruda if
the truth be known, oh well, i
know more about jim thorpe and
franz too, who once asked me to
see him buried beside the big
indian . . . drunk tho he was, still
another pledge i've broken, but
what could you do, against family,
collectors, men with money or
power to move it . . . anyhow, more
about these than about trains or
you, or indeed even my own father
who rode the commuters' local
every day even if business was bad—
but i remember we, then, were
hooked bad enough we went down
to ludlow station, why?, to watch
the twentieth century—and the
pacemaker came through, i think
at 4:17; and, also, from either
station house high over the tracks or
the railroad bridge a half
mile down, or even from the

embankment between, we played
our games and watched to see
the trains come through . . .
and from the same high bridge once
we pissed on some late afternoon
locals, boys whose peters hung
themselves out beyond the bridge's
edge and arced the fine streams
for all we had to offer—but
never no rocks thrown as now i
find they do, well, then
they were friends, the iron horses,
we loved them best, better than
the tugboats on the hudson, or
the amphibians overhead, better even
than the hindenburg they pulled us
out of school to see pass by one day.

we used to argue whether 999
still ran, and hoped one day
to see it. and, pablo neruda,
in the circled front of ludlow
station one spring day a man
approached my father, mumbling
in italian. no capeesh my
father said, and in such a flash
i found him linguist—the
yiddish and german i was used
to, it was expected, but here,
eyetalian, and then it turned
out bastard french too—all from
three months at orly field, 1918—
my own father linguist (like
learning uncle bob a member of
the lost battalion, or another
uncle in the fighting sixty-ninth, i
called bobby klein immediately . . .

II

    neruda it just seems
    to me all our fathers
    die poor dirt farmers,
    but some were railroad
    men, some had some
    piece of themselves to
    hand you on, a big
    gold watch the printers
    gave my granddad, gompers
    shaking his hand, or my
    poor father, when the
    central was a train that
    ran on time . . . the boys
    whose fathers were railroad
    men, they're getting
    fewer—trading off for
    astronauts, oh

    casey jones.

LESSON I

for c. o.

Runs
on any dirt diamond   blind
man, intent
on next bases,
not the ball.
Fifth element: luck;   said Johnny McGraw
without coaching has no man an idea
of position, no knowledge of ball's placing
Without coaching the base runner is caught off his base
the runner is kept from the plate without coaching
Runs do not go up on the scoreboard
runners make no advance under flies
the rallies are squashed inning and inning
from the first, even till the ninth
The Giants are not without coaching
Neither the Yankees, both first.

THE FOURTH ARK ROYAL

for e. d.

    time is an old lady
    like madame defarge

    she sits weaving us
    into it, humming old
    tunes, tunes we half
    remember, or somehow
    haven't heard at all
    we say: gee, what are
    the words to that, or,
    what's the name, damn
    it, or, how does the
    rest of that go

    we say what we can, is
    the simple truth of it,
    as if there were
    simple truth wherever
    time that old lady
    enters in. she will
    not be true to you,
    and she will not be
    true to me, she is an
    old lady concerned with
    the pattern she is
    weaving, only every
    stitch is true, and
    might even have saved
    nine

        so we come, finally,
    to a bar. there are
    old friends, the women
    are beautiful, someone
    has money, the drinks

flow and flow, we talk,
in the end, that almost
comes to be the best for
us, that we talk, what
else were we constructed
for, even?

          in the quiet
light of early spring one
comes on strange things in
bars, the other night it
was those young sailors
from the ark royal, the
fourth, i had to discover
by asking, talk again.
they thought the
first fought with
drake against the armada, the
second was in line with
nelson at trafalgar, the
third went down in the
north atlantic. now
the fourth sits at anchor
in new york bay, and
the young english sailors
flood ashore, they are
all over the city, even
in the cedars, asking:
is that a beatnik, and for
once honestly asked, they
ask as simply as if the
question were:

          what time
is it? or what is the
name of that tune? they
are here tonight, too, in this
bar where old friends are
meeting; helene said:
every time i look up there

is someone else i haven't
seen in eight years. what
is the name of that tune?
then we come to where we
have nothing more to
offer other than our bare
souls, and the old lady
giggles as she knits, she
thinks she has us there
but this is what we have
to come to, i keep telling
myself; what else to offer
an old friend, no gift,
not money, sex, liquor, not
an old suit, my cousin
eddie does that for me,
not even the graciousness of
our presence, christ, might
as well have a dinner
party for that. half
remembered what we have said
in the past beats as
firmly against us as the
pulse in this night's bourbon.

i thank you for it, that
a memory beats again as
solidly as you walking to
the platform, your feet
set solidly (your feet
set solidly in a different
way, of course, than
mine) i saw the pace and
thought what tune is
that? what are the
words to it? and how
does the rest of it go?

we have beat the old
lady, and that's the

loveliness of it, sometimes
you do, even if she
doesn't know it, keeps on
knitting, weaving in four
ark royals, young
english sailors, your
kids, my kids, tunes we
ought to have remembered,
tunes that never did
exist, tunes that shouldn't
have existed, too many
drinks, and some drinks
that were perfect for
their time, our friends
gather round, we even
bowled a game, the perfections
of a grace directed at
the limited world a game is.

what tune is that?
how do the words go?
what's the rest of that tune?
this i want to give you
to take with you, send
me answers whenever you
get them, i'll tell bob
too, and charles and max,
whoever in this world of
ours might be listening,
one of us may find out,
if not, we haven't lost
anything . . . as if there
were anything to lose we
haven't already come onto
and made a decision about.

i'm sorry three ark royals
had to go down, planes from
the third crippled the
bismarck as she dashed from
the denmark strait trying
for france.

                and even
this has no bearing, until
we give it one, whatever
it deserves. my friend,
i offer you a drink, my
bare soul, and a half
memory of when we last met.

and i remember best that
time is an old lady, like
madame defarge, somehow
weaving us all in, humming
old tunes we might not
remember, at the door.

POEM FOR LOUD LAUGHTER

for p. w.

'ends
1,000,000 miles in
orbit'
    and, so
easily let down,
gently, caught by a
cargo plane 'in
center field'

          gently, gently
          we need no
          concern with gravital
          formulae, or the
          pisan tower, galileo
          extending himself

that simply caught up in
nylon ropes, nets, hooks
reaching out to grab, grapple
the thing into place

the proper place, isn't
that what we're always
concerned with?

        ha, nylon
nets, hooks, grappling,
the whole damn thing another
hassle in the hay too.

and they used to be silk,
silken, the nylon nets, and
the panels of g–8's
parachute, too, 1937 or 8

the paper's practically
crumbled by now, they used
so much dryer in the ink.

'the nose cone only slightly
burnt'
      it's easier to
say that the man selling me
bourbon has his own nervous
tic, twitch and jerk of
the lips, running up as far
as the middle of the cheekbone—
he won't let mr assistant take
the cash but rings the cash
register himself, mr ben zeeman,
he's growing a beard, two
weeks old, the stubble clear on
his chin, the line of demarcation,
as clear itself.

      and it is warm
for november this late, and
there's been no real frost so
how can it be indian summer even.

but i do believe, thinking abt it,
the smell of burning leaves does
not fill you with the same as
my security, who fought fires
differently—houses in north
carolina the extent of which was
digging in the cherokee halfbreed's
house's cellar to find his
granddaughter's doll, the one
she couldn't do without.

no smell of burning leaves
there, tho there was more
than a hint of something
else, the old bastard refusing
completely to put up with
the white man's ways, no one

will ever know for sure whether
neighbor one or two did it
or he himself to lay the blame
on them. in any event, that
somewhere between the fires
of leaves burning along park
hill avenue or hawthorne back
in yonkers, and yours, on
top of that mountain. a
different smell leaves burning
smelled on top of a mountain
when it's your mountain and
the leaves are burning.
                              i.e.,
you laugh that loud, you've
learned something about
when things are funny.

A POEM IN TUNE WITH ITS TIME

for c. s.

anything else would be frivolous,
at three the house filled with
smells of stuffed cabbage for the
queen of the sabbath, at five the
damned goyim fish smells, frying.
anything else wld be frivolous, not
the dream caught in napping, anima
suspended and held by the hand, she
led you down the waits and days of
nights.

    what color hair yours got?
or, your anima takes numbers.

THE ACES

for g. s.

> *. . . his delights*
> *Were dolphin-like; they show'd his back above*
> *The element they liv'd in . . .*

never having seen cars race,
i still believe in nuvolari;
that somewhere in whatever
guinny heaven exists, he is
there, cornering before god.
and he is still hacking away,
coughing his blood out inside
and outside the machine, so

much blood in that man, he's
still spewing it in that heaven.

and behind him, in the dust,
the big yellow deuses, and the
white auto unions, and the green
british cars, and the cars whatever
color the frogs were driving,
they're all spinning off, losing
wheels, but nuvolari is still
driving hard, cornering, all
the way home.

       and next door, in
a different country of that
heaven, there's a nice level
piece of pasture, eternally,
little and stubby, but throbbing,
the winnie mae starts, tail
beginning to feel the air.
wiley post waves once, and is off.

he died in the air, and
nuvolari got it on the
far turn, against the
wall, spitting blood, but
still leading, twenty or
thirty years after he should've
stopped.

       and the eighty-five
year old stonemason said:
so what? so what if i go
blind? i'm an old man.
i seen plenty.

POEM FOR NEW CHILDREN

for a. and l.

world, before us like a
bride, we will enter you
gently as we can

           driven,
driven by needs past
what we know, that fearful
pressure

        we enter you
lovingly, though we cry out

world, as when love is
new, we are sure we will
satisfy

QUADRIVIA

for j. c.

there are waterfalls pour
straight down
           i will not
say they are boring.

buttermilk, on the
other hand, cuts its way
down the palisades, fights
a little, it is a thin
stream, it always shows

white
     i suppose because
i was sleeping on your
side of the hudson, because
there was a painting
before me, and visual
images will determine
simple reductions the
mind moils up

          the eskimo
does not make this jump,
the eskimo jumps by other
means

     my father lies sick
across the hudson from where
i slept and i have not
gone to see him either

he sends me postcards

he tells me i will click

if done properly one can
drink a fifth of bourbon
in a day and remain perfectly
sober

they are taking more than good
care of my father, and
each waterfall finds its
own way to the sea

LA REVOLUCION

for j. s.

blood red the rust from
the pipes runs in
my tub, then thins

later, beads
of water diamonds on
the hairs of my
forearms

i have no food in
this house, i have
two glasses to wash

diamonds on each
hair the decorations
of a king

       the forearm
bare in fall, summer
is over

       i will wash
the two glasses, i
will drink, outside
there is food, it is
easy enough to get, if
one have the appetite;
we make our own beds, then
we lie in them, we
sleep
summer was a hard time
we did not all of us
make it

       we took our
baths, we swam fresh

water or salt, we hiked, we
saw the waterfall, the
main stream, and the one
fine line of trickle far
to the edge
         streams have
run blood red too,
but that is not
our concern, we have to
make our beds, wash
our glasses

         the diamonds
glister, each hair
holds its own diamond

in which realm then
i am king

LOVERS

N. B.

love is not memory, love
is the present act

is what have we done for
us lately, is where
am i, or you

you are sitting on a
rock in the moonlight
your red-blond hair
loose in the moonlight
you are crying

that was a long time
ago. a lot happened.

and if her hair sitting
before me is the same
shade, rarely found,

                      your hair
is not love, love is
the present act.

NEW BLUES FOR THE MOON

for d. d.

i know your door
better than i know my own.

and ought to warn you
i bring habits into
every house. dirty
laundry here, supper
there, a quart or two
of beer, wine, whiskey.

the habits a man is
constructed of, ought
to know himself by thirty
if there's any good to him.

to you. and still haven't
figured out how a woman
walks. my last duchess
had small hard nates. this
is a different matter.

infinite variety in a
grain of laudanum.
infinite variety in
by god what are you doing now.

i know your door better
than i know my own.

CLAMS ON THE HALF SHELL

for m. m.

like the baroness, a
new outfit every half hour.
like the baroness, higher
than a georgia pine.

you'll come to him fiercer
than new grapes, the skin
thick enough to split itself off.

the bite of the juice a little
bit acrid, the seeds solid in
the flesh, almost impossible
to extricate without losing it all.
these were grapes i ate from
an italian's vine, in brooklyn,
so the fruit is vivid enough, the
dull film which covered the skins.

anyhow it had always seemed to him
fruit the female element. the biologic
necessity, the form and shape itself.
ripe, neatly halved, the inescapable seed.

A FIVE ACT PLAY

for b. j.

one more kind act the
world i've constructed
won't exist. one more
kind act i'm liable to
be able to move.

                      one
more kind act i might
straighten out, stop
scratching my toes, yes,
one more kind act baby
i could cry and laugh i
mean really all those
lovely things a man is
made of.

            one more kind
act i will i mean i
really will, baby.

PEIRE VIDAL AT THIRTY-TWO

for m. k.

but i thought i
loved her, and what
was love, and what
was she—that i thought
i loved her, and what
was thought? doing in
all that, and where
were the spring flowers,
why should they have
any part of it, love or
my thoughts, better to
concern myself with the
breakfast i am cooking
and eating alone, better
to concern myself with
my dirty laundry and
my garbage, who else will
take care of that, i
ask you, all the while
thinking i had loved her.
or her. or her. or her.

A LOVE POEM

for m. s.

like a flower grows, i
think, out of a green
stem, but then i don't
know.

    or, in the sky, the
stars grow pretty big, i think.

so then, like a flower growing out
of a green stem, i come to you,

or you are, i don't honestly know
which. the stars big in the sky
express something, about us; you
tell me. didn't you think so?

other images also come to mind,
like the sands of the sea. or beach?
the poem consists in the fierceness of the onslaught.

FLORA

for j. g.

wandering jew even
your one purple
blossom gone, now
only the green and
purple leaves aglow
in the evening

you keep on growing
yet she swears every
other plant died for her

once every sabbath or so
the purple flower reappears,
now on this branch, now
down there on that one

the simple and insensate
act we all live by, one
purple flower
              you are
composed of all the green
leaves you could dream of

ach, i make too much of you

WHEN WHAT YOU DREAM

for f. e.

i am concerned with impossibilities, the
old man walking too slowly across
second avenue, impossible notes from
impossible people
                  if the check comes
                  you can give it to me
                  or h- at the cedar bar
                                        j-
i am concerned with impossibilities, the
way the sun crept slowly and steadily to the
fourth window. the dream is perfectible
and sometimes everything else falls before it.

it's that i'm getting old and tired i
would guess, gaining something in each
instance. in each crackling log we steal from
ourselves to throw on the fire we learn something:
it is burned up, it is consumed,
weigh the smoke and the ashes, you come up
with the weight of the log that has been
thrown in. the fire crackles merrily, damn it, it
is the least efficient fire i have ever
participated in, or warmed myself before.

start again. if the check comes—and what the
hell do i care for him anyhow, a friend of a friend,
and not even his friend anymore, walking out of
the drug store with a forty year old whore on
his arm, fell for his horseshit: he's waiting for
his check, and me, like a damn fool, i give it
to him. better go to jail for forgery than
give him his check.
                        what does this have to do with it?
something about the dream, his
was the check, at least for last night.

                              and if i didn't
know better i'd say brandy was good for the soul,
but perfections count for nothing, and the
imperfections are what i depend on.

II

on groundhog day
on groundhog day

he might be dirty but he's got
a real fine sense on groundhog day

on groundhog day

it's too sunny
i think we will have the
six weeks of winter.
you were right
not even seeing the sun
there's too much of it,
but when you're awake anyhow, might
as well get up, the weather
won't change, but
you're through with sleeping, on
groundhog day, on groundhog day

A CLOWN'S COSTUME

a clown's costume is made of
diamonds, and the hat is
fully lined. the dotted
material will fringe his
neck, his hands also come
out of a frame of it. a
shame a man has to come
to this, and so old, too—i
wish he had run away to it
a million years ago. we
could have used a clown then,

things weren't so funny.
infinite patience is required,
my dear, to make the points
match up right, fine work
with needle and thread. the
poor clown clad in
diamonds, poor clown, his
heart is breaking it's
the same old stuff. i
hope he gets good and drunk,
and the young tightrope walker
falls in his arms with love.

i hope the costume moves him
up, out into the center ring,
emmett kelly used to walk
around it fighting the spotlight,
trying to sweep it up. and
almost got it. a different
kind of classical costume . . .
pantalone, harlequin, scaramouche
sabatini added, i remember that.

whichever isn't my color, or
the right side of my face.

concern yourself with it, the
impossibilities of a rich old
man cavorting at grossinger's in
a clown's costume, sewn carefully with
grace and precision.
i hope he enjoys it.

IV A BRIGADIER GENERAL'S UNIFORM

this uniform is constructed from
the finest shoddy, government issue

'how do you know so much

                              about the civil war'
                              'i read'

                         lies, all of it

lies, they are not only burning
my letters, they are burning my
pieces of wood in their fires, in
the evening by the meadow i can hear
their banjos playing. they are burning
everything i am or hope to become,
and in time they may even grab you under
a misapprehension

                    'we regret to inform you
                     your daughter was
                     burned in a fire not of
                     her own doing due to a
                     regrettable misapprehension'

my god, what am i talking about.
my god, why not walk around in a
brigadier general's uniform, i
ask you. if you meant me to be
a brigadier general why don't
i have wings.
                    no epaulets please,
let it be simply shown on the
shoulder straps only, the single
star, as the sun is a single star,
as the sun shines merrily along, a
single star. let the saber even
be tarnished, let there be a dead
cigar clamped between the hirsute
lips. oh you know who i'm talking
about, what difference does it make.
it could just as well be the old
professor from maine, governor of

the state, president of bowdoin.
that's what happens to heroes, i'm
afraid i won't make it, even if
i had the residence requirements.
do you have to live in maine to
be its governor? i think so.
i think i won't make it.
                        meanwhile,
i swear to god, the band is
playing a sousa march, and they're
reasonably in tune. the eidetic
image will destroy all of us
some day.

V

the band plays merrily, you
are leaping into summer, you
have a red flannel nightgown on,
none of us understands anything
about warmth, only of fires, sun,
red flannel, that's what it
comes to. and i thought i
would study it, make myself an
expert in the subject, get myself
a bachelor of warmth degree.

therefore be careful what log or
leaf from dining room table you
lay on the fire, it may burn.

in summer, keep warm, this
is important. let the cold do
what it wants, since i learned it
could kill you it doesn't frighten
nearly as much. i.e., you
know what you're up against.

as in, he thought, war pictures

charges keep being made against
the unassailable enemy. ah, that's
closer to it.
        'the long drawn-out losing fight'
          that's very close to it.

        it might even be why i
        know so much about the civil war
        and the band playing sousa marches.
        now they are cheering.

do not send to know for whom they
cheer, they cheer for you, sitting
in front of the fire. simple
enough. careful work with
needle and thread. i can't go on,
the costume is falling apart. and yet,
that night, she said, it was all of
a piece. how do these things happen, threads
gone awry. they happen. simple enough.

if i could say it to make any sense, i
would find out eventually what the
sun's about, these days. the cheering and the
tumult subsides. pack up your fires in
your old kit bag. throw another
log on the fire. when what you dream.

Philip Guston 1968

from IN TIME (1969)

A PRAYER

oh, the word, and the
bloody wine that
changes it. the
bloody wine that is
my body. the word.
the wine. the body.
they move in circles,
stalking each other,
hunting, hunting, feeding
on themselves, on
each other, no one
gains, no one loses,
save one's own sense,
one's own sensibility.

was it camus talking? one
writes to find a reason
for living—i am
living to find a reason
for writing. and
existence banks on the
ability to exist—the
simple ecology of the
soul. we are all incapable
it seems of living in that
environment we were created
for. we are sea turtles
who don't really like
salt water, or condors
afraid of heights.
                    we
hunt ourselves, being
unwilling to live by
other laws of nature.

the word is: to thine
own self be true. and

we lie. the word is out.
the bloody wine changes it.
and the minister says
the words and everybody
bows to them.
                   and the
weather hangs over
us all in a poor season.
not even able to live
with the weather! no
ease, no flow of life,
no song in the words, no
song in the wine, no
song in the body. the
poem does not exist, the
poem does not *work!*
                      we
swim in the garish salt
sinking, we climb on
our mates for sustenance,
we support ourselves in
an alien atmosphere, using
every handgrip there is,
and we do not fly.

the blood flows thru
our veins, and the wine
thru our mouths, and
the words thru our
heads, our muddled heads.
give us this day our
daily word.
                and let the
bloody wine leave it alone.
let it grow on its own,
let it flower in its own air,
let it have body. let the
word grow, and be a sustenance
to us, now, and in the hour
of need, let it sustain us.

LOVE

IN THE BEGINNING

i have few clothes and
many books, you bring
few clothes and many
books, still, have no
doubt of it, the one
closet won't be enough,
and tho in our world
there is always room
for one more book
somehow the clothes
will be a problem. tho
in bed there is no
ending the combinations
there will not be room
in one closet for two
suits four dresses two
raincoats two winter coats
and your new spring topper—
if they still call them
that—and the shoes, my
god the shoes, what in
hell to do with all of
them, not even a plastic
shoe bag hanging on the
door of the closet—we
will move to a bigger
place, two closets, lugging
the books and the bed.

A NOTE

in the touch—if
not there, not
at all. head and
heart open and
close in their own
concerns, skin only
does not lie or
delude itself. the
hand reaches out
while the mind
considers, the
hand grasps while
the soul adds it
up. the hand
rejects or accepts
while all the rest
play games.
                it's only
a game the rest says
while the hand, furious,
is furiously involved.

FOUND ART

if what one were about was
writing haiku what
else would one do filling
time between seven-
teen syllables neatly

spaced
      what i meant to say was
i like the way things happen
sometimes and you and
there we were looking at
a yellow sun over the
river and perhaps
grasshoppers or herons or
daddylonglegs chirrup-
ping and the sun yellow going
down, i said what
had to be said and the
sun went down someplace
else where we didn't even notice 'til
outside the window it
was dark, but inside the
window not even a
football game not even
a haiku disturbing
us
   what i said was
i think i'll name
the universe
and you
and did
and the sun kept going
down, where?, over
the river we
weren't no more
grasshopper heron or
daddylonglegs watching.

THE POEM

they have returned
the wrong
letter.

A VALENTINE

the shape of the heart
transplanted is in
question. the only
fully working organ
i can hand you is
a well-oiled elbow.
i sit sipping and
think how my liver
swells with gratitude.
and you lie in my
bed, and i have not
determined why

nevertheless there
is a thing called
love whatever the
shapes, as just now,
irritably, i said
i can't keep an
eye on him while
i'm trying to write—
loving, like they
say, the facts of
both of you.
             he

was formed in
your belly, he
walks now, stumblingly,
and sometimes falls.
one or the other of
us picks him up
to kiss him. occasionally
i reach for you in
the dark night. sometimes,
too, i turn away,
curled in my corner
of the world. what
curious shapes. but
then, valentine's
day was never my
holiday, rather
groundhog day, in
which my nose pokes
curiously out to
test the universe.
i have found you in
this annual excursion
and am now content
as possible, given
the hostile world, and
the more hostile organs
of my flesh. i know
you understand this,
which is why i call
it love, despite the
shapes it takes
love. the heart.

SWEET BLUES, AND OTHER SONGS

I

and that sweet
joining where the
thigh meets hip

the socket of
desire
     oh yeah

nothing like it
on the subway
any-where

     she
fussed with her hair
as any maiden would,
everybody off here's
where i get on, that
sweet joining where
the hip

II *(proverbs)*

meat to eat, or
one man's person
is source for
the gander. the
nearer the bone
the neater the feat.

III *(explication du texte)*

roll
misery
roll
you ain't

nothing
but a bed get empty feel so mean and
blues.

IV *(the old-time brag)*

i got a chick gives
out for kicks
and i don't care about
this shit

i got a chick gives me
pussy for kicks, ain't
gonna work no more

V *(the resigned and joining blues)*

that would be, effective
two weeks from

i'm resigned you i'm
resigned i got those
sweet joining blues

sweet joining sweet
joining
      where the
hip meets the
hippest of them
all, in the

socket, oh that
socket

of desire.

THE MIND IS THE EASY WAY OUT

if it were only
green moss. that's
how i think of it:

green moss

green moss the color
maybe of terra verde.

a simple mantle of
green moss, i could
tell you what god and
man is. green moss growing
over all the rest

a rich warm deep color
green moss the color
i wish it was, i could
lay my head down in the
lap of it, relax. green moss.

POEM IN PRAISE OF PERSEVERANCE

i suck at your
tits, eat your
pussy, fuck in
desperation,

        some
call it madness,
but we call it
love.

only the grey hours
get us upset about it.

i.e., there are
times neither of us
can stand it. there
are times we each
jump out whichever
escape hatch avails
itself to us. do

you remember the time we

and other popular tunes.

MODERN TIMES

wind rattles windows.
my lady abed, myself bare-
legged out of poetry.

the cold wind. slow-
ending winter ending.
february, and the paper
insulation in the
window half-ripped out.

and see her on her
elbow in the bed.
she is reading, and
i, at my table, i
am reading also.
and i will have to
say we have recently
made the double-backed
beast, tho wind rattle
windows, in the end
of february, in the
end of winter, with snow
yet to come, and hard
winds and hard rains.
we have made the double-
backed beast, and warmly, too.

this much
will a little quiet do,
and peace, in our times.

LET ME GO HOME WHISKEY

when drunkenly i groped you first
in the back seat of the car that
was taking us drunkenly swimming
in the moonlight drunkenly and
found there bare tit to kiss and
further groped the cool mound
also bare, naked under your muumuu

in chandu did kublai khan a
stately pleasure mound he found

naked under your muumuu i went down
on it or as best as could there
in the vw i hoped you liked that

and the swimming christ it were
cold, how'd you expect to see
a hard-on that way (i knew a guy
went mad trying to fuck a
abalone all one summer, one he
was in love with, but the abalone
wouldn't open up save in water
just too cold for him to keep it

easy come or easy go) but there
you were even more naked than
under your muumuu, and then you
started talking to the fucking horse

BLONDE LADIES' SONNET

well, i will break myself once more against
your slender blonde-ness. i have learned no way
but that. i, like all men, was born to haul
ass after beautiful women, and knew
no other goal to assault, assault being
the right word, since you too my love suffer
in this campaign, believing as you must
i am warm passionate jew, blood running
hot all through me, and what you will find
is the image of the image of a
man making love to the image of a
woman—images whirligig about.

against that slender beauty, blonde, i break,
and still, in breaking, never find mistake.

KEEPING IT

fourth day. work.
man sings a song over
and over; now the
president is singing it.
the world we live in
is not what we sing,
and we are afraid we will
fall prey to that we
are most afraid of, the
truth. the truth's a
bitch must be whipped to
kennel while my lady the

brach sits by the fire
and stinks. let us now
praise famous men. or,
it is a bad time for ladies
to be beautiful, how will
they handle it? work
is the same. how will
i handle it, me, like
wallace stevens, an
executive. but no
secretary, no crumpled
copies of poems for her
to copy off. i love
women is the story, i
love women, though it
rives me though to admit
it, though it steals my
sleep to admit it, though
it shakes my bones to admit it.
the song i sing is the
truth, it is the simple
declaration of the
faith a man must have,
in his own balls, in
his own heart. i love
the shape that is not
mine, that fits mine as
the glove the hand.
this is the faith we
live by, for our
women or ourselves, if
we live by any.

THE CLASH

when i was fifteen i read spenser.
two weeks later, in a poker game,
drawing kings over queens, i named
it *the bower of bliss*
                     this knowledge,
of course, came far too early, yet
how was i to know this
                     and now i have
seen women do terrible things, and
known myself also—i have come now
to so many terrors of the clash between
us i do not know what i believe, and still,
and still, and still.

THE NEW STANDARD SIMPLIFIED AMERICAN CABALA FOR HOME USE

ivory box, you
rest in my safe, locked, and the
ruby
    no one sees.
the earth stops moving
in the small death, you have
swell legs i see now.

another weekend gone, the
poem not written, the piece
lost in the shuffle.

THE SURGEON IN SPITE OF HIMSELF

last night, put to it, shaking
hands and all, made a god-damned
surgeon of myself, picked up the
sterilized table cutlery, there
in the middle of the atlantic,
raging in its own impossible gale,
performed the neat cut, the
careful excision, and the suturing.
my hands still shake, it
is still the atlantic ocean,
and it is morning. i
am almost afraid to look at
the patient or the sea, but,
master of my own fate and captain
of my soul, i know that i will.
as i know now to otherwise live
in terms of my necessities,
it is fervently to be hoped.

A LONG WAY

in new england
the winter is cold
the spring too abrupt
the summer hot
the fall keeps creeping up on you

what the women do is beyond me

the men, two or three years
on the boats, carving, that much
we've seen: whalebone, ivory,
driftwood, anything attackable
by knife, scrimshaw strewn in
the windows of the bank, as
someone collected it.

someone else, a warped
mind, no doubt of it, working away,
collecting the others, dildoes,
whittled, carved away, love
messages running down the
main vein, the head intricately
doodled, even a double handle
at the base on some, they had
those too, invented the better
to hold on with. at each leaving,
left as a gift, a blueprinted
penis measured somewhere south
of the equator, laid out in
bone or wood, a solid remembrance
something to keep her
                      better than

burning with desire, i wouldn't have thought
of it, here, myself, in the city.
and, didn't, indeed, 'til told of it.

a hand-carved dildo, somewhere
in our own sargasso

YESTERDAY

this morning plum
incense burns in
the house, and the
machinetta hisses
gently three times,
so the coffee is
ready
      and we are
reasonably convinced
all the nuts have
gone to far climes;
we relax
      the gulf
we were swimming
turned unseasonably
warm. what started as
the desperate attempt
ends a vacation at the
sea. they are serving
wine melon balls and
crab, not to mention
plum incense or
expresso
      and tho all
our ideas are foreign,
and floods and scents
also, finally our
stroke is our own
in said gulf

SUNDAY MORNING

the idea of
the mind handling
the things of the
flesh. it's this
which upsets me in more
rational moments . . .
and i dream of other
times when we
lived another way, not
even knowing there
was another way where
men hung themselves
up, steadily.

THE BRUSHES

a tenacious man
he hung on, he
hung on, that
is, his fingers
clung to what he
had to cling to.

if he had not, what
could he have clung
to in order to sit
around all that
time. that is, the
involvement necessarily
that which life is

made up of, either
you hang on, or your
fingers loosen, you
drop off, because
it's no longer worth
hanging on to it, what
you were clinging
to, that would be.

did you understand
that? while your
fingers were tightening
around? the bones
of them stretching
themselves clinging
to? as to a rock
in the middle of
the ocean? in a
great painting by
watts, hope sits
on a rock in the
middle of the raging
ocean, desperately
fingering her harp.

a tenacious man, and
clung to what was necessary
to cling to, tho fingers
tightened tight as bone
can tighten, tho the
flesh between the knuckles
wore away, tho the knuckles
themselves, showed bare as bones
to the sunlight beating down, on
the rock in the middle
of the ocean, clung to it.

he was a tenacious man.

SIX-DAY AND BALL-BEARING

riding my own, having
to pump harder going
downhill than up, it
won't coast at all.

if i said to her, i
stink, she wouldn't hear of it.

round and round, round
and round, just for the thrill
of it. competitiveness.
a suit of clothes to
the winner of the next eight.

listen they don't make them
like they used to, stamina
enough to beshit yourself
even in public view, if
it meant winning the race.

even then, if i said to her,
i stink, some hero worshipper
in the third balcony would
lean over, shouting, say
it isn't so, and i'd have
hopes for my future again.
still, the bottom of the
hill is both start and finish.
keep pumping, sir.

THE THREE AND A HALF MINUTE MILE

love ends neither cleanly nor dirtily
but out in the open, in an italian
funeral parlor, tho you may not
believe it, for the stench of the
gladioli pervaded that room so bad i
could gag on it, and the obsequious
ushers nearly got kicked in the ass,
and i saw myself patiently lifting that
last stone which must be dropped over
the part where the head is to make
absolutely sure the ghost won't walk.

and it was so young and pretty, it
is a shame.

        love walked right in,
circled around the room, and died,
right there in full view of all the
admiring public, cheering it on to
the three and a half minute mile.
and neither of us cried, tho in the
movies we ought to have, painfully.

save the gladioli, gardenias are a
corsage i got for a blind date at a
fraternity dance in bridgeport in
nineteen forty-seven, and violets, that
spring flower, are what i wanted to
see sprouting in your snatch.
he picked up his carton and left.

ZEUS, IN MAY, REFLECTS ON A RECENT LETTER FROM ASTARTE

as if it weren't what we had
always asked for, the new
season, the sun back in the
sky, flowers, flowers all
starting up again—the
spring king went and did it
again, gave himself up for
the greater glory

                and the
season does change, and
we change with it, now suffer
a sunchange: the skin opens
itself out, we can eat in peace.

my dear astarte, whose mother
was it you wanted to be? don't
fight kiddies, eat up all the
chicken soup—it does happen to
come to this dear. i can't
even say i'm sorry for it, tho
i can commiserate if that's
what you need, over my bowl of
yummy oatmeal without any
lumps even to stick in my craw,
over the perfervid image i
carry somewhere in my gut
and try again and again to
make come forth perfect.

THE THREE OLD LADIES

      what is it in me won't
believe that which i
am or not
          hears the
voices of pretty
women, smells them
out to hold them in my
lap, where i stroke the
curves of their asses and caress
their bellies.

         love, you
come to me in the strangest guises,
and i suspect if i asked
for a valkyrie, you would
wear turkish harem pants.

and who wants, after all, rum
napoleons on five hours of
sleep? who wants somebody
else in your space, chattering,
and the shakes from last
night's drinking, and, for
that matter, who wants the
pressure of a hard-on, whether
in the flesh or the mind, and,
yes, who wants the girlie
magazines stacked neatly by
the bed?
         there are other
definitions, i know that.
if not, mortally offended
one might pluck oneself out.

THE ECONOMY OF ART

every sunday nite it's
the same whether you
eat well or not at
all, whether you drink
heavy moderately or not
at all, whether you nap long or
short during the day, or
not at all, still you
lay down to sleep and, four
hours later wake to a
cold sweat and clutching your
lady's tit to protect you from
the ogre monday morning.

ZOO STORY

olaf the
walrus at the a-
quarium—remember that
the adult walrus can
take on polar
bears—was for so
long swimming there with
seals only, when they
finally came up with
a lady-love-to-be, and
put her in (tho she
was not yet of age, quite).
it took hours before
he knew her for
walrus even. then he

clutched onto her, and
held for five hours.
the keeper, then, fearing
for her strength, had
her taken out.

walt you sing of
yourself

THE NEW NIGHTGOWN

i believe you, i
believe you. but
tho you be the fool
and me the hanged
man, let us both
transfer to magician.
it would be nice
to run our own world.

what else is there
to offer you or myself,
save myself as
man—as for you a
self as woman you are—
and about this, we, like
others, over-read, under-
read, do every damned thing
save live.
        the way out
is via the door; how is it
no one will use this
method? confucius asked
a long time ago.
                put pants on the piano legs,
                secret holes in the nightshirts.
                have two women all over you, or
                three men. the body has apertures,
                the hands and the tongue reach out;
                why is it we so rarely satisfy or
                are happy ourselves? this is no
                simple question of potency, it is
                mass communication in the raw.

shall i say that if i
had four cocks they
would be for you—but
would solve nothing for

either of us that is
not already solvable
by other means. as, if
you had four cunts all
for me, what would i
do with the three
others? i am trying
to talk to you three
days before i pass out of
christhood or alexandrianism,
and i am sick unto death,
again, with judaeo-
christian graeco-roman
shit. i want you as
i never raved before—
and still can't talk
straight, or touch, and, yes
still drink.

> "she was coming on to getting
> married age and she stay out 'til
> five one morning. now you know
> she got to have a red belly then."

what, i keep asking, do these
have to do with us—and
know how tightly tied all
of it is with every hard-on
i get or every wet pussy you
find yourself with. and, too,
the elegance of the new
nightgown—tho our angers
flare and rage it may be there
the answers are—in elegance,
no cop-out, simple statement.
what power implied!
what power to tap! only
one cunt necessary then, only
one cock. and the rages part
of it—it's mine goddamn
it, leave it alone! as,

sometimes, blindly lashing
out: i hate you mother-
fucker! well why not?
if there is strength to
sustain it. if i can stand
being loved i can stand
being hated. that simple.
and to act simply in time
of trouble, that too. i
will fix your bra the same
way i go to work. as i
think to present my life
to you, the simplicities,
complexities, inanities,
unswallowablenesses.
there. there. there.
how shall i touch you?
how reach out? how
lift up my hand? how
lay it tenderly? how
roughly? how meaningfully?
by lifting my hand and
reaching out tenderly
roughly meaningfully.

the way out is via the door.
you know she got to have
a red belly. i'm to
have an axe again. i had
my dick all along, as you
your sweet cunt. why is it
no one will use this method?
let us not forget elegance.
let us make some simple
move to satisfy ourselves.
let us attack the central
problem of desire, by
desiring. nympholepsy,
that rapt state induced by
craving for the unattainable,
if it must come to that, but
there are better endings.

i hereby firmly resolve
to try to reach you as long
as i want to reach you.
what a reasonable fucking
statement, without even imagery.
the other rules are:

        never be martyred in you own bed;
        refuse to answer any questions you can't;
        you can't fight a revolution without love;
        fantasies ought to be discussed.

i reach out to touch you and
find flesh, which sometimes
disconcerts me, that's where
our world has gone to, this
time, i didn't know that was
what to expect. and am
conscious that kissing your
tits i remind you that you
are a woman, as, if i get
an erection, it is to
fuck you with.

        ceremonies
        exist in
        the mind

        ceremoniously i
        undressed and
        dressed you, then
        the air changed.
        it became real
        instead.
                but

        ceremonies still
        cannot be damned,
        well used can
        indeed make sense, and

        can move to a
        different reality.

i wish it would
all happen at the same time,
and we would know it.

US

A TREATISE

friends
go, disappear, do not
return, are lost, and the
cities stay on and on.
nations at least in name
change, but what the
babylonian has left, the
assyrian has taken, what
they left, the medes and
the persians, what they
have left, so on up to
the turks; now
baghdad is in iraq, and
it is still baghdad, there
is still a mayor tho
not haroun al-raschid,
it still destroys the
souls of men, it is still
quick to rise against
any people in it it
thinks threaten it, as if
man could do more than
threaten this golem only
man and the ants and the
prairie dogs make, a
city, friends disappear
in cities, or they go
out of them, some of
us sit and watch from
our windows the great
going out, if joshua
were to appear outside
the walls, say just
off the washington bridge
one of our girls might
allow him the information,

but we would sit on
inside, alive or
dead, because in the end
the city is addictive,
you get to need that
sickness running thru
your whole self, as sure
as you need to get drunk
to sleep, as sure as
you need to pass by every
misery that shows itself,
you are not the caliph, you
don't fake yourself at
night and wander out
among your people, you
do it another way, you
are out for the main
chance, even love is
difficult in the city,
tho you destroy yourself
hunting it, it is all
that is worth hunting
in the city, unless you
want the pleasure of killing
rats, even the love of
little girls to be
hunted in the city, that
poor bastard, all these
years mad for little
girls, what do they think
the city does these proper
bastards who have never
lusted after anything,
never given themseselves
particularly to their old
ladies, who have never
felt the city sitting on
their shoulders, have not
felt
all the buildings lining

fifth street towering
down on him, he speeded
up his pace hoping to
make second avenue before
he was pinned beneath all
the tenements, christ yes
that is the city which has
existed we know since at
least 4800 b.c., they
dug up those ruins, the
shards of "the first city,"
damned agriculturists, even
for the city the farmer
has to take the blame, as
i come to think for most
ills we are heir to,
damn abel anyhow, cain
knew what he was about,
and god too, he marked him
then in his sin, but cain
saw it coming and made one
valiant effort, it wasn't
enough.
   7,000 years of
this madness, 7,000 years
of man tied to the
city, the only reasonable
alternative would be
hunting and fishing and
quite a while ago we outbred
that possibility, oh yes,
now, they tell me, the
government is moving the
indians off the reserves,
into what? mill towns,
factory towns, the
ultimate end of what
the hanging gardens
were about, mene,
mene, tekel upharsin,

you have been weighed
in the balance and
found wanting, of course,
did you expect to be
satisfied in the city,
this dull slough, where
blues is all in your
bread, and poisons too,
and no taste, bread is
no longer food, we had
that fight, tho he wouldn't
believe it, but it isn't,
not in the city, bread
is not food, god knows
there is little enough to
live by in the city,
bread isn't one of the
things, and yet the
city exists so the
farmer will have his
markets, or the merchant
his port. i prefer the
ferry landings used to
cross the great rivers,
there were no cities,
a man and a ferry, a rope,
perhaps, across to haul
him along by, on
such a ferry masai was
able to cross the father
of waters on his way
back, st. louis however
disturbed him profoundly,
only the hunter has
sense enough to be
upset and confused and
therefore to leave, the
rest of us sit quietly,
waiting for whatever,
secure in the knowledge

baghdad still exists,
and only a total war between
nations ever destroys a
great city completely,
pouring salt over the smoking
stubble where people
once lived, and even those
cities thus destroyed grow
back in time, and the
people are the same or
different, but that doesn't
matter, what they wear, what
they speak, what they
eat, all that matters is
the built-in mechanism
of self-preservation of
the great ba'al into whose
maw people are thrown
not knowing generally
that they carry yahweh
inside them and don't
need false gods, time
and again, jerusalem
destroyed the jews,
it is doing it again,
and yet jerusalem goes
on, an object for
everyone from nebuchadnezzar
to colonel nasser, the
knights templar, and
saladin. what then will
my soul do but fred
thompson's act, but
not overtly, rather, hidden
in the dark recesses where
not even a wife would
find it, where not the
city or agency thereof could
reach and pry, where
the city exists but only
as a shadowy menace, and

we are enabled to act,
otherwise there is no
peace, or too much of
it, too easily . . . or
there are a few other
external choices, if you
must go that way, the way of
geo. metesky, so many years
of filtering bombs into
this city his hate was
so huge, or the other fellow,
angel i think his name was,
no, august robles, him,
holed up in east harlem,
fighting the police, when
they got into the room,
one of the detectives stood
over his dead body and
pumped his automatic
empty into his dead head,
each shot tearing something
else out of us. they had
all given up the idea that
friends would return, that
love was possible, and the
farmer who said, sometimes
you can't wait for love,
it would take all year, he
was talking of the bull
servicing the cow, that's
it, the perfect word,
servicing, he had won again,
the market was quiet and
busy, everyone was back
to business, the city
was at rest, there were no
more circles on the
pool from the thrown
stone, the stone was

buried, dead, at the
bottom of the pool,
the pool was closed
over, not even friends
would know where to
look for it. and are
there names in potter's
field, or even, possibily,
by numbers they count
them, every man his own
auschwitz, what else the
concentration camp but
the perfection of the
city, what else the ss
but the perfection of
the state, what else
the factories and stores
but lesser gas chambers,
and they let you wear
your watch, they do not
remove the gold fillings,
but they do give you
your piece of soap, you
are going to the showers,
and baghdad is now in iraq.

THE HEART

likely the lions swing
their weighted tails by
waterholes, the gazelle
eland and other creatures
pick with care their way.
but the gorilla i think sits
on its haunches psychotic like
in the zoo beaten to such a
state to guard the keeper
bringing it its food.

WHEN THE DRUMS STOPPED

he dreamt of himself
a leopard and lion also
reasoning satan and redneck
man, a duality of
nightmares that wrecked
his sunday night and
monday morning. the lion

fitting an arrow to a
bow impaled the leopard
to the lady's door. he
wrenched the arrow out
and slid away, into
whatever existed outside.

oh reasoning satan, oh
redneck man, the earlier

dream had woken him saying,
oh reasoning satan, redneck man.

the arrow bit deep inside
him, yet, he found, if the will
be there, it can be torn loose.
who will stanch such wounds,
the blood wells slowly.

in the forest find poultices
of moss and mud, lie
in a thicket where they
will not follow. if the end
should come this way, he
woke once thinking, the
end comes, and that is the
end of that. the pain of the
arrow he heard the twang of
the bowstring echoing all day.

and yet, and yet, redneck, satan,
leopard, lion, souls of romance,
there was a lady's house, there
was a lady stood inside, nor
cowered to the leopard or the lion,
pitied not, hated not, wanted
not, only waited. how then to
rationalize this out. sing songs,
dance, drink or otherwise, you will
still have to enter that house, fit
an arrow, twang, be impaled, save
the lady, escape, come to the
house, receive your reward, hide
in a thicket to come on, another day.

AQUARIUS

in february the
water runs slow
under ice
      carrying
the spring, cold
and clear the
weather starts
its turn around.

aquarius strides
sky, water buckets
in hand, he will
pour them, the
land comes awake.

fruitful one,
builder, creator
spirit. an old
man, wise now
he has learned.
it is water we
need. water.
all other things
die or can be done
without.
      water
makes life. and
the ram, the bull,
the twins, the
lion, the virgin, the
archer and the goat
need it, the fish and
the crab live in it,
the scorpion in his
dry desert needs little,
but needs some, and

the scales are
useless without a
man to use them.
                    pour
it out old man, make
spring for us, make
life, make the poem
spring, and the
painting, turn the
dipper deep so the
water plash down,
we will run naked
in it, great rills
of water bucketing
down our bodies,
the warm air just
around the corner,
the love blooming
in us—or else
carry us in your
buckets, given
breath, given life,
carried to godhood,
old man at the
beaches of heaven,
old man scooping
the sky for our
sustenance, our poem.

THE LOVING MACHINE

rose tits jam made of
rose tits, ass to be
flavored with love.
knees shone white in the
moonlight. breasts were
those of the *kora* i knew.

as glory do!

as she rises notice the flower
of love opened beneath you
no cunt but a fucking
geranium glistening
beneath you.

WRONG AGAIN

according to the latest
report in *the times*, the
backside of the moon has
only one cheek. i did
not want to know this,
venus de milo being
bad enough.
              li po, in
the depths of the
yellow river, making
love to the moon, did you
not discover this? did
not your hand at some

point stray round, gripping
her tighter, only to discover
nothing?
        all men who have
lusted, full moon or
no, wouldn't this
finish it? diana, how
could you do it, artemis,
how run properly thru
the woods, selena, i
hate you.
        i shall return
to persephone, earth-
grown bitch. even with
her problems sitting all
round the house, at least
her ass is complete! at
least in this she does
not deceive me.
        and,
li po, i am drinking a
sad drink to you, who loved
as well as any man, but
loved the moon, i am
sorry for you, this sad
drink for all poets who
in drink or not mischoose
the target and then aim
too well. may the emperor's
favorite concubine come
once again to you, disclosing
by the chinese moon her
alabaster ass and hold you
close, closer than the
yellow river or the yellow
moon could ever dream.

THE TRAVELLERS

you, where you are, ensconced
in a high plateau. you are,
you have written, hungry for
"uncommitted free time." who
is to blame you? having given
as any of us your eight hours
daily to the traffic, and your
night's bed to the visions
perquisite. now you have
loaded it all, the children,
your wife, the gear necessary and
unnecessary as well, the books,
onto an old truck, you have
slid easily through utah, no
more indians to beset. you
were in the desert, have gone
now to the highlands. i am
still in the city waiting
for god knows what, but i have
chosen it, tho houses such as
yours, and in other places, too,
beckon and wait . . . i seem
immovable as a statue, even tho
there are women in all these
places, drink, and food also.
we, at least, knowing each other,
will not begrudge our ways.

may all who travel, travel lightly,
eat well, and find sleep nightly.

THE INNOCENT BREASTS

the innocence of her
breasts. the way in
the soft morning, as
she leaned over him,
reaching to see the
time, they hung tender
and innocent.
               just
six hours earlier, as
in many other beds,
they had been hard
and passionate as
pomegranates, and a
few hours before
that, every man at
the party wanted them.
go further back: ten
months ago they had
been filled with
milk, and the boy
suckled, and the
man held back his
hands and lips—now
they were not his.

we are all, we know
now, bone-pickers after
darwin, rag-pickers after
marx, brain-pickers
after freud—we are
trying to reconstruct
our history. breasts
are a sexual attribute.
the chimpanzee's flat
chest with long nipple
is more efficient for

feeding. the breast is
a sexual attribute. they
hang warm and innocent
in the morning.
                    four
hours later, at the
forum, fortunately or
not, those breasts took
over the conversation.
after all man is a
political animal also,
and can figure a way
to breasts even with
war. but she was embarrassed,
saying, they're not
even that good. and he:
you didn't think i'd
mention your ass, did you?
and the politics of
breasts leads men into
madness, tumbling over
each other in a
mad race for a
sight, touch, taste.
i won't be blamed
for it—unabashedly i
stare through every
see-through blouse,
look down every low
neckline, peer carefully
through the right
kind of armhole. it
is nobody's fault, we
are born to love them,
even though they are
difficult to make
love to.
            the buttocks
at least are truly
functional, allowing

us mobility, agility,
speed. the breasts hang
innocent in the morning
light. at night they
tighten in desire; in
the evening they peep
provocatively. the
young man asked plaintively
whether lenin had ever
wondered about the cup-sizes
of fellow revolutionaries.
i hope so—this is how
the revolution gets
made.

     in the morning light
he ached to touch them,
catch the weight and the
softness in his hand, but
could not. some obscure
idea made him just watch,
while she thought him
still asleep. they were
too innocent in the
morning light. he thought
it no time for the carnal,
though he laughed as he
thought that. he preferred
the thoughts he was
having, to the action—
not perversely, but as
a special delight.
          besides,
after the forum, they
would nap, in the warm
afternoon, and the meat
of it, the true carnality,
would carry them. the
breasts hung innocent
in the morning light.

SEIZE THE DAY

the Old Woman sits at
the Window all day. She
can't Walk or do much of
Anything. almost every
day Russell visits her. he
sits at the Window, too.
When Russell is Big and
Strong he will Carry the
Old Woman to the Circus
to the Ballgame
to Meet the Queen
Everything she's always
Dreamed of.

17–18 APRIL, 1961

well at last i am done with it
and the dream is over, america,
you and your dream, once and
for all you have finished it
off, in the voices of my fellow
workers, workers! shouting not
paredon which would be alien
to them, but, to the wall, straight
out in good old american, to
the wall for all who disagree,
all who march in times square for
whatever they believe in, america
you have come to think the cops
know best, you have come to think
the bourgeoisie, the druggists, the
tradesmen grand and petty, the
dealers, are to be trusted as if
it hadn't been proven time and
time again they would suck you
dry without thinking twice, without
even being capable of knowing
they are doing this, or knowing
they are doing this, it comes
out the same, the bourgeoisie
who know they are dupes of the
big money, and the bourgeoisie
who do not know, the
big money as remote a thing as
liberty from any of our lives and
yet in control, there is not one
man who rose above himself in the big
money did not in the end buy off or
kill, somehow destroy.
                    remember, america
eugene debs said he would not
lead you into paradise if he could,
because if he could lead you in,

someone else could lead you out, that
was the text you ought to have
listened to, that was the text you
ought to have believed, instead you
bought a world free for democracy,
and you bought a return to normalcy,
and you bought a new deal, and four
freedoms (freedoms you might only
have, anyhow, if you look deep inside
yourself where all freedom is to be
found, and not with rockwell hands so
carefully and badly drawn . . . and then
america they will be unnumbered, un-
countable freedoms inside you, america).
america yes the square deal and the
new frontier.

our friend mr. stevenson stands up
and speaks, he is either a simpleton
they have not told anything to, or
a liar; which destroys you more
america, which is the more terrifying
thought? and the liar from the soviet
union stands with evidence in his
hand and i did not hear one word from
mr. stevenson about that evidence, only
what our master of eloquence chose to
term "a categorical denial" which is
no denial at all, which is worse even
than pleading the fifth, and you know
america how americans feel about their
constitutional defenses by this time,
you know america how many are hung
each day because they take the fifth,
america we have brought you to the point
where it is better to lie and hope not
to get caught, than to behave honorably.
well, this has been true of the world
all along, but it was not supposed
to be true of you, america, here

was supposed to be truth and justice,
here.

    and yet even so there were
signs all along, the big money
burned benedict arnold and he went
to the bigger money then, the big
money took ethan allen and battered
him down, he chose to sit out the
rest of the war, the big money did
not like what mr. paine might say,
and he paid for it too, the big money
fought and beat or bought all of them one
way or another, and some they killed . . .
let's not talk about it, the big money
is always there, you were supposed to
be bigger than it, america, sometimes
you almost were too, think of andy
jackson fighting and beating mr.
biddle's bank, and better yet, two
terms later mr. tyler in spite of his
politics came to feel some of the
greatness of america in the president's
seat and would not restore mr. biddle's bank.
but oh how many battles have you lost
for each one you won, america, are they
enough to balance out? i think they are
not; finally i am through with it, with
the american dream, a dream that ran through
all my ancestors who fought here for you
america, and i still grew up a jew in
yonkers new york, forced constantly to
blurt out historical fact, great grandpa
carried a minié ball in his leg i would
say, and feeling the sickness in me when
haym salomon was praised in ninth grade,
and all this shit, and still i was a
jew in yonkers new york, america, don't
misunderstand me, this a man can put up
with, this a man can learn to live with,

roll it off his back sometimes, until the
breakthrough comes, but this is only part
of what is bothering me now, this is, in
the end, my own problem in my own soul, but
the problem in your soul is that 63 years
after mr. mckinley we are still fucking
around with dreams of empire, we still
cannot bear to let people work out their
own destiny, we still cannot believe in
keeping our hands off, we have forgotten
we once carried a flag into battle that
read don't tread on me, we think we have
the right to step everywhere, we are free,
and therefore every other man is beneath
us to be trod upon. i will not do it,
america, i will fight my own battles with
my own enemies, but i will not have the
police and the cia and the fbi and whatever
other force you dream of america protect
me from my own heaven or hell. america,
the list goes on, do you know, up there,
you will not let me kiss my lady's cunt,
you will arrest my lady should she kiss
my cock, we will both be lost if i am
caught carrying her on my hips around the
room, some places here in america you
will arrest us if we fuck in any position
but me above, and her below, and by
god don't enjoy it or perhaps you
will arrest us for that too, item:
did willfully and with malice aforethought,
have, and cause to be had, a pleasurable
orgasm, yes america this is what you've
come to in this year of grace.
put a coinbox by my bed, then,
america, i will pay tax each time,
put a coinbox in my skull, each time
i think a treasonable thought, each
time i conspire with myself to advocate
anything mr. dulles, mr. hoover, mr. any

body else says i oughtn't to, i will
drop coins in, a surtax on my own
personal albigensian heresy, a far
worse heresy now, because it is against
the state, and not just god, poor
god, what dreams he must have had for us,
and now i feel as sorry for him as did
noah, job and jacob; i will write a
grace for god:

> all that that i have done
> i should not have done
> all that that i have not done
> i should have done

america, we have been telling you
all this, and i know that you did not
want to listen, well, that's fine,
no one said you had to, or, for that
matter, even should, that's the difference,
that's what america is supposed to be,
where you don't have to or should, but
i am just reminding you you did not
want to listen when allen yelled at you
like jeremiah, you did not listen when
charles patiently explained to you what
you had done to gloucester, you don't
listen even now when ed tells you how
it is about charitable clothes, you
will not listen to me, but still, we
are covered, we said what we had to say,
each in our own way, america we have
indicted you. i do not think,
america, you will ever be able to produce
the shakespeare to write that history
for you, because i think america by
then, a hundred years from now, you
will have succeeded in creating a
people even orwell couldn't have dreamed
of. my grandchildren will be part of

them, too, that is something else to
hold against you america, truly.

am i, america, to tell my children
not to fuck, to spill their seed like
onan on the ground? how else then
to prevent it, they will have children,
and america you will turn them around.
i think too much about it, i know,
this is my weakness. it is a common
enough one, or used to be; america
you are not letting this weakness be
common enough, it is too easy to teach
the other way, everyone knows that;
america you were supposed to teach
each man to think, you were not supposed
to supply an economy which exists solely
in terms of how many cars are made out
of how much steel each year, you were
supposed to base the economy on something
reasonable, god knows maybe even food,
the simple damn potato, the bean, corn,
wheat stored in surplus warships, that's
what you were supposed to do, who
could ever give a damn about a car unless
it were nuvolari driving it, cars are
for perfections, like any tool, they
are not what we are supposed to live by.

l'envoi:

now you are patiently going to explain
that mr. castro is a bad man and needs
a spanking, and impatiently i'm going to
tell you what i thought, all along, poor
fool that i am, what i thought the american
dream was was a world in which two wrongs
don't make right, where we threw out the
window fighting fire with fire, christ a

nation of petty inventors what don't we
know about fire extinguishers? you've
succeeded america in trading it all in for
the damned idiot who'll stand up and shout
once too often my country right or wrong, my
country, my god how can any country be
your country when it is intent on beating
down everything in it it once stood for,
when it keeps getting wronger and is happy
about it, america you have a sin of pride,
you think you are better than the russian
tanks rolling through budapest, america
forget aguinaldo, forget the indians, forget
the slaves, forget all that, just, for
once america, admit it, stand up and admit
you have killed everybody who stood in
your way, quickly, to the wall, rarely,
more often america, the slow stewing in
the prisons and the reservations. and
you keep on telling them you love them.

when you have admitted it, america, then
you can give it up. america you're no
better than any of the rest of them,
and i'm sorry for it.

PUBLIC AFFAIRS

what's all the shouting about, the
man wanted to know; i couldn't
tell him.
        it wasn't, even, as if
there wasn't anything to shout
about, there was plenty, i can
tell you. but how could i translate
successfully enough? to tell him
just what the shouting was about.

so, finally, since he kept insisting,
i told him all, how the celts had
deserted their sacred oath, and more
important, the border guard, and

alexander, big man, halfway into india.

POEM IN DEFENSE OF CHILDREN

liberty to be defended on
foreign shores so that our
children can be safe and free
would seem on the surface to
be reasonable.

        not one man
who says it will defend his
child himself. let me stand
with a gun at my child's crib,
whose name is the gift of god, the

helpful one, let stand over him
his friends, guardians, parents,
let each opening of his fists,
each start at a smile, each
try at turning over, be covered
by me. it is not my business
that another child burn so
mine shall live. it is not
your business. it is nobody's
business.

      or put it this way.
that woman in black pajamas
with babe at breast is evil and
abominable, while my wife with
my child's lips sucking at her
is a holy thing.

          defend your
homes, your wives and families.
no one else can or will.

            defend
your lives so that you can
sleep at night. defend your
souls. defend that truth
that is your one inheritance,
or crawl, and cry, and kill.

DREAMS OF GLORY

our rightful place,
astride horses at the lead.

jongleurs beside us. i
saw the swords flashing, heard
the words of the songs we shouted.

a lady's garter belt
hung from my braces. i
thought we might have enough
pipers, too, to march us through
the marshy ground wailing before us.

i thought there would be trumpets also.

goddamn wednesday forever.

POEM

the kings march and the
men march. a man lost his
sight on iwo jima; he is
drawn, sightless, by eight
more veterans. in the middle
of paddies gooks are hiding.
they have no purpose but to
lurk and kill. americans
are dying.
         pilots fly out
of guam, piloting b–52's.
a b–52 is a powerful plane.
liberators swirled and died
over ploesti. twenty-four from
fifty-two is twenty-eight.
die american! buy american!
the plane dips and swings,
the pamphlets drop over
illiterates. bread is
plowed under.
         "i wish"
the pilot said, "those
fairies were in a paddy
one hour!" i wish he was
in a paddy one hour.
         my
friends, for whether or not
you believe it, we could
be such, since we could
certainly drink together,
and have, my friends, i
am sorry you have been put in
that position, where the gooks can
kill you! where the gooks
can hide and kill you!

while your generals and
your people, most of them,
believe you're being
cheated! where the whole
military mind refuses to
believe that men fight to
defend bunker hill with
shotguns and old muskets,
that men hide behind trees
or up to neck in swamp
to win a battle, that men
fight and run, firing two
shots at the officers,
men who could kill a squirrel
at forty yards. which side
are you on, bo, which
side are you on. sevier's
men came out and surrounded
the mountain at night,
killing the good king's
men passionately because they
came too close to home.
pitt was damned, the
people supported the troops
wheeling with brown besses,
dying damned heroically
to hold a fief not sworn.
men die, the kings keep
marching, people back
the wrong horse noisily,
killing themselves the
things which let them speak,
and it is not the blind
veteran my fight is with,

but the old warhorses, who
have never done their time,
but know what's good for
us, and gooks.

THE RIDDLE

what's gray and comes in quarts
is an elephant or my brain;
what loves or walks slowly in
the land is an elephant gray
and old, they have waited a long
time for her to give birth.
what i am saying is the age,
we live in, we grow old in,
grayness is not a state of mind.
you have red-blonde hair, another
is black, and there are jews with
orangey hair from the east of europe.
come to whatever you come to slowly.
haste makes elephants gray before
their time, routs the bears from
the caves before their time, turns
the leaves before their time, only
the weather should control the
climate.   where else are we but in
this parallel, caught between our
own isobars, read the temperature,
make sure it has numbers on it
when it comes out. what's gray
and comes in quarts is a joke.

A FABLE

the ring of it then,
the somehow noise it
made going off
            the
hanging up of
everything all at once, that's
what it ought to have been.

but the bull don't know
a thing about dramatics,
he just reared up his
self almost erect.
far off in the
corner of the field, old
lady friend
far off in the corner of the field.

THE PRESENT

in the gray mist that
early dawn what else to
discover, man, you lover—

                this skeleton has a rib
                "punctured in a way that
                appears as if done with a
                sharp instrument"
                            the other?
                homo neanderthalis, 45,000
                years old and you're still not

                    out of it: you have the honor,
                    like a world series record,
                    the oldest known amputee, his
                    right arm appears to have been
                    manually removed, above the elbow

my bully boys! my bully boys!
done him in, and the dawn dawned
bright and early, a trifle gray,
there wasn't even emperor or king—
just the flint knife tied to the
wooden shaft, not even spearthrower
invented, not even the goddamned
sword, just the spear shoved in, or
another knife, sharpened a bit
differently, ground rather to a
broad flatness, tied to a short
club, blade laterally, to be brought
down sharp in the hacking swing,
a good clean blow with the axe, tho his
people managed to haul him away.

and when cro-magnon came? he
could do it better. good enough
to do you in, loutish, chinless,
flatfaced little bastards. the
women were small and muscular.
as a people they spread all over
europe and the near east, maybe
even further—and disappeared
almost in a day, done in, and
have never been heard from since.

dawn, dawn, dawn, if it gets any
lighter we won't see a thing.

DEAR MISS MONROE

everyone else is writing you, why
shouldn't i? i mean sometimes you
look lovelier than any human on
earth, at such times my heart
goes out to you. believe me
marilyn if i married you i would
never write a movie for you, even
though i'm a writer, and while
interested in sports, i would never
once hit you a home run, i mean
that's the way i am, the type of
fellow, and the way i feel.

you might like to know, however,
a little more, viz: when i wake
up in the morning, after smoking
a cigarette in bed, and then
peeing, i perform my ablutions,
first, generally, i wash my, no
first i take my vitamin, then i wait
while the water warms up, and then
i wash my hands, and when the water
is warm and my hands too, i wash
my face, and then i dry my hands, but
not my face, unless it's tuesday and
thursday (on those days i don't
shave) and then i put on the lavender
shave cream from the shake-em-up bomb.
while that's setting, i brush my
teeth with my fingers and colgate,
as my gums won't stand for a
toothbrush any more, even though
i've bought a soft bristle one.
i also clean my glasses at this time,
while the shave cream is sinking
deep. then, after drying my hands

again, and my lips from the tooth
paste, i put on my clean glasses and
begin to shave. up until 1:35 last
saturday i had a chin beard, but now
i only have a mustache. shaving
around the chin area is not a
happy subject these days as it is
very tender. i mentioned this to a
girl the other night, as she happened
to caress me there, on the chin.
after shaving i wet the end of
the towel and use it as a wash
cloth to get the rest of the
foam off me. it smells pretty bad,
i don't think it's really lavender,
a house brand from bloch's drugstore.

that's how my day begins, on those
days when i get up too late to do
anything but my ablutions before
going to work. i go to work
thirty-five hours a week.

if you promise that your real
image will be the same as your
image on the screen, i probably
will want to marry you. i am a
sports-loving jewish intellectual
writer. some nights i think, while
i'm in bed, of how lovely your
body must be, and i don't mean of
when the king's hand is sneaking
under the sheets while you two
kiss, i mean of when you and i
would kiss. thank god i'm not
interested in tits any more, yours
would probably drive me out of
my head. i think i could stay
sane enough with your ass and
belly though to make you reasonably

happy. or else i could write a
poem for you, for your birthday
or our anniversary or whatever.

i remember the story about you
and mrs. miller at pesach, the
one where you said after five
nights, mrs. miller, every night
we have matzo ball soup, is that
the only edible part of the matzo,
the balls? i want you to know
i have told that story, and many
times too, but i never once believed
it, i just told it because it got
a lot of laughs, but inside i hated
myself. i wanted you to know that,
somehow it seemed important
to get that straight.

other things i promise not to do
are: that i won't shoot rabbits
that are eating our lettuce unless
we need the lettuce to live off,
but i hope that will never come to
pass; 2) i won't ever buy canned
horsemeat for dog or cat food, although
i am now going (she thinks) with
a girl who has two cats, and though
so far it's been only tuna fish and
eggs that she serves them, who
knows what she might come up with
next; 3) i will not convert or
attempt to convert you to anything
except more and better me, this
seems fundamental in any marriage.
i want you to know also that i miss
my kids too and could conceive of
such a dumb stunt as gay pulled that
night, sentimentality and all.

this is the first poem i've ever
written on my new electric machine,
marilyn, so i must also ask you to
forgive any typographical errors
that creep in, due to my unfamiliarity
with it. the people next door are
getting restless, also, it is late at
night, so that may cut short this
message. in any event, when you
looked at gay in the bar when he
was talking to you, my heart melted.
it's corny, maybe, to say so, but
gee i sure wish you'd look at me like
that some day. i think something
might come of it. do you like to
drink? i only ask because i like
to drink overly much, like they say,
and would hope that once in a while
you might like to get stoned
with me, instead of me always
going out getting stoned
alone and in secret, or even worse,
having to get stoned with you all the
time. that is, i would hope that you
are the kind would like to get stoned
once in a while with me, and sometimes
would let me get stoned by myself without
getting too bugged about it, but, in
general, that we could plan on going
to bed sober, say, three times a week.

the thought of going to bed with
you reduces me, at this point, to
a jelly, but i am sure that, faced
with you, in the flesh, as it were,
i would forget that you were america's
beauty queen, and mine, and would find
the wherewithal to produce. i hate
putting it so baldly, but you must
understand by now that this is a problem

you face, i.e., you tend to destroy
any man facing you by psychological
warfare. that's probably what happened
to arthur, but that's his problem.

i can only say again that i think i
might learn to love you, and would
certainly cherish the opportunity.
i am at present engaged in polishing
up an essay that is due in two
weeks, and i really must stay with it,
as my tendency is to fuck off whenever
possible, but i certainly would like
to see you if you will be free any time
after the twenty-first, which is when
the essay is due. i will try to write
you a poem in the meantime. yours
very truly, a secret admirer, joel.

LIFE AS IT IS LIVED

no zoo anywhere in
the head, the heart, to
compare with the actual fact.

:   the giraffe, the
rhinoceros—even once
to see him raise himself
upon his legs and move.

to touch a goose.

to ride a camel.

                    : bumpity
as hell, the little boy said.

**THE 150TH ANNIVERSARY OF
THE BATTLE OF NEW ORLEANS**

andrew jackson, now my
lady has pasted the new
orleans stamp between her
breasts, so i feel you
are honored. who never
had much problem with
women, duelling over rachel
not so much for her or
your sake as for the
needs of silly pricks

as the men at the shop

didn't know whose profile that
was stood high on the stamp
for the blood it cost.
as they were arguing later
whether d.c. was a state.

as i hate all men who don't
know where they come from.

as i feel you honored because
my lady had the sense to lick
your stamp and paste it there
between her tits, proud
as you yourself were, and
chic as posting riflemen
in swamp up to their necks—
god knows we won't fight
that way again, ourselves.

between her breasts that high
head rests, hair upstanding,
sword outstretched.
                      andy
show then all. once
a free man ruled the free.

i pray god in peace he sleep,
and his angers find release,
and rachel's breasts in joy do leap,
and we americans find peace.

PASSING THE TIME AWAY

i fuck you
i fuck him
i fuck her
i fuck it
if uckt hem
ifu ckth em
if uc kthe m
and that's the way
i tg oes

THE LESSON

seized by
sickness, the
implacable body
reacting the
only way it
could, not
knowing anything
except the
foreigners to be
expelled, the
mind with no
control—this
is the frightening
part, no
control, no way
to say: stop!, no
way to ease the

spasm, let it
run its course
painfully, holding
on to pipes, tub,
the bowl, let
nature run its
course, the body
will protect
itself, tho the
mind be
terrified and
have nothing to
hold onto, nothing
to judge the
force of this
reaction by,
nothing to allow
a peace of
mind, this
time only the
separation made
much too clear,
the body and
the mind, in which
the body only
will take no shit.

BRONXUS

people around here all
the time walking their
dogs even at seven in
the morning Leave it
alone don't walk your dog
so much
    it'll
fall off my sainted
mother might have said

STUDIES IN ARABIA DESERTA

giving what you have on
short notice my friend would
seem more valuable than
knowing what to do—god
knows more useful, at least.

getting through hard spots
is hard going is an old
chinese proverb, or russian,
and finding a hand is not
always the easiest either,
or being able to take it.

why? because it's there
said sir edmund, and now
the americans have done it too.

and if we wander into deserts

or swamps, they're there too,
and what the hell is there
anywhere in this damned place
but earth air fire and water,
maybe a hand. take it. you
will become richer. you
will start to look for oil or
natural gas. you will start
again building your fortune,
your fate, you will even
start thinking of love again,
a human relationship, you
will think of those women,
friends' wives, with their
bellies swollen, and you will
find them blessed, and predict
handsome children. men live and
breed and eat and build in
tents on the desert, in caves
on the edges of mountains,
on stilts in the middle
of swamps, and they make it.

EDUCATION: THE MUSEUM OF OUR YOUTH

hang them up on the wall, the
poems you've written, it
doesn't matter. it doesn't

even matter my dear friend
if they possess him yard and all.

hang them up on the wall even
if only for esthetics they'll
bang away at them. every man
a critic that's the way the
world goes. they'll all tell
you how to do it, and be amazed
you keep on doing it. ever
try to screw with van der velde
looking on? or shoot yourself
up next to rimbaud? look, what
we need is a museum of our youth
so we'll remember where it is
we came from.

                a complete set of war cards

                john w. gambling on tape

                the interior of the sacred
                heart church gym where you
                learned to make those flat
                set shots they don't make any
                more always hooking up the
                looping arching ones dropping
                in

                the double bill allegheny
                uprising and elizabeth and essex,
                we played that one in the lots

three weeks. in a crystal case
the tears spilt over the biscuit
eater, don't deny it

how milk used to look, two
inches or so of yellow cream on top

one wallet still preserving the
oval press the trojan sheiks or
x-cellos made in the fine brown
alligator, always in readiness

the knotboard—hang it on the wall

a complete and definitive description
of how to position yourself at the
door of the cloakroom so as to jab
a tit with your elbow

don't you forget them, and
don't get hanged when you get home.

AFRICAN MEMORIES

for the watutsi in their hour of need

they are fighting, she
said, on the beaches, etc.

and on the left flank, a
small detachment of batwas,
poison dart blowguns eveready
as batteries. for three centuries
the bourgeoisie held subjugated
to the artists merely because
of height, the lovely air
one breathes when one is
seven feet tall. keep them
down, damn them. but are
there beaches in ruanda?

listen, all over the region
the drums are beating, bahutus
rage, seethe, form into
companies. the lion invented
the assagai just when napoleon
ravaged the continent. hah!

where were the bahutus damn
them when humphrey sailed down
the river? and needed them,
even to some fermented honey
beer to replace the gin she
poured away, bitch. but they
sank it anyway. altho the
koenigsberg did make it upriver,
that was somewhere else in
africa. nevertheless the krauts
dismounted the twelve-inch guns
and hauled them inland, to become
the last german force to surrender,

weeks after armistice day.
so there they are, spread
against the indian ocean, the
arabian sea, the mediterranean,
the south atlantic, fighting
all these years away. but for
three hundred years the artists
were ahead, by virtue of their
impossible height, and the togas
they wore draped shoulder to hip.

arise! formez vos bataillons!
on to the dark continent!

THE FAKE SMILE

O Jung, O Adler, O Freudian, shrinker of heads,
Give me in due time, I beseech you, a little goyishe-kopf,
With the little bright wishes piled up neatly within the ego
and the loose vagrant libido and id,
And the bright super-ego noosed under the bright bone brain-
   pan,
And a way of thinking not too queasy,
And the ideas dropping in for a thought or two in passing,
For a hip thought, and to make me my share of it.

O Jung, O Adler, O Freudian, shrinker of heads,
Lend me a little goyishe-kopf, or provide me with any obsession
save this damn'd obsession with loving, where one needs one's
   balls all the time.

POEM ON THE DEATH OF WCW 3/4/63

now you are dead
no more to see
flowers or women,
no more great
mullen in jersey
salt flats, now
you are bones that
three-legged
dog can worry, now
you have eternity to
consider those mysteries
your life was
built on, now, if

like marc antony you
too are listening in
heaven, you are even
permitted to laugh
at all of us working
in your woodpile, where
you knew enough to
settle anyone
          —and yet, you
          were always a loudmouth, did
          it have to be so silent, and
          you who of all of us knew
          the waste of news, how does it
          happen i hear of your death in
          the middle of music and

and yet i know what men
are saying and what men
will say, and i know
what the burying will be like—
but what of the river above
the falls, and what of great
mullen and the city itself,
what will they have to say?
when we know that yesterday
was supposed to be sunny and
warm, and suddenly it was
gray and raining—what
to make of that besides the
usual inanities about death?

old man you will be
missed! old man
you will be missed!
you will be missed by
children not even made
yet, ears not even
thought of by any young
man walking the paterson
streets—and there

you are, with only
asphodel as you said it
would have to be—oh, christ, yes!
death comes to every man
and we are supposed to be
happy it came silently, it
came after long sickness, it
came while you still could
write a poem; and happy
it waited seventy-nine years—
well, that's just not
much to settle for, old man, and
i think of the poems still
coming, couldn't talk,
could hardly make the
typewriter work, and the
poems still came—

thank you old man
                for all you have
                given, and thank
                you old man for
                all you made yourself

A MAGAZINE

> "One can learn from Lewis and Clark
> that the Missouri nourishes
> cottonwood, alder, cypress, lynn,
> coffee nut and the oak, and yet
> be sluggish."
> Edward Dahlberg
> Because I Was Flesh

sometimes the culture
goes bad, rioting
under the microscope;
the affair gets
out of hand. sometimes
the culture spoils
itself, tho the lab
be kept pure as can be;
or, there on its glass
slide, it breeds its
own destruction.

                    i would remind you the
                    scots bards were the
                    only members of the
                    clan forbidden to join in
                    the battle. even the
                    piper carried a claymore,
                    but the bard must sit on
                    a height, recording.
                    someone had to be left,
                    even if the clan were
                    destroyed, to preserve
                    its history. the
                    culture was trying
                    to save itself. but
                    then the scots were,
                    as far as i know, the
                    only people of recent
                    date in the west, who
                    put the richest in the
                    front lines, with the

    peasants in the back.

    i beg your pardon,
    but i seem to have
    wandered back to
    war again, it is
    hard to avoid these
    days—so we will
    talk about affairs.
    another curious word
    indeed, whether of the
    heart or state, or
    catered or foreign.
    affairs go on all the
    time—we are sitting
    at one now. and
    a magazine is where
    they keep the bullets.
                      bear in mind, let
                      this magazine be where
                      the bullets are, sitting
                      on its hill, noting
                      the affair. someone
                      has got to tell us
                      where the art is, now
                      that we know it exists.

                      somebody has got to
                      tell us where the
                      money is, now that we
                      know that exists.

    art & money, he said, we
    should name it, and i
    countered with lux et bux,
    but in any event it
    exists, and i hope
    it flourishes. this
    culture needs it all,

art, the dour testament
of edward dahlberg,
the stern musics and
the happy ones, the
dance, the very movement
on the slide beneath
the microscope, the
culture growing, bubbling,
the culture springing
new forms, forms not
inimical to life. we
have enough of those;
now it's time to grow.

MATHEMATICS

we come to another place.
there is no reason we
stay one place only. there
is no inertia we cannot defeat,
and we are going to the
market to buy vegetables—
didn't you know that?

we are those who have
never once admitted the
validity of the hair on
our heads no matter how
strongly we have praised
that beneath our hands.

we do not now talk in
terms of love or even
position, we talk about
problems in the calculus
of motion. how, in going
from here to there, do we
intercept or not intercept
that which is going also

        i have drawn the map as i
        drew it then, the dotted line
        is the line of march, the bluffs
        were very high at this point

        severe cold
                (i.e.,—28°, contrast
                scott, shackleton, lieutenant
                greeley)
                        many
        cases of frostbite, the general's
        ears even. the general doesn't

    like fighting indians, he wants to
    go south, where the glory is

    shan-tag-a-lisk, spotted tail, with
    such a name, given such a language,
    might not you ask the general if he
    would name himself in such a manner
    as you have: bad medicine?

    spotted tail, and you, the big mandan,
    neither of you may ask the general
    anything, you may stare and glare across
    the line of cavalry, you may watch
    the two howitzers, and behind this screen
    you can see the eighty pawnee scouts,
    they are staring over at you—they
    at least you can fight, they have names

we talk only in terms of
the world we see, whatever
we talk about. we are not
now talking of love or of
the laying on of hands

  "The rock bluff was limestone without fossils . . . .
   heavy growth of very large willows here, quite tall
   and some of them two feet in diameter, with very
   heavy underbrush of willows. From the mouth of White
   Man's Fork down to this camp was twenty miles . . . the
   river bend and the bottoms were about five miles wide,
   covered with high rank grass . . . ."

seeing the world—oglala
is a village divided into scattered
bands; brule is burnt, burnt
thighs, they were the riders

tho it was not a simple
journey we have come to a
world the real thing that

simply; it is after all
a hard world to live in

now we will learn anew how
to move ourselves. it will
require the devising of the
particular travois necessary
to this undertaking—see,
already we have found the
willows necessary, a "very
heavy underbrush of willows."
and without horses we can use
the dogs, who will also do

OLD STORY

a man was out walking his
totem one day and
got lost
     *but the
map is not the
territory* he kept
screaming. neither
was the territory. and
tho he invented fire and
bent his opposable thumbs and
laughed and constructed
memory, he sat there alone with
this big goddamned bear next
him.

    when the woman found
her way to that neighborhood
she was in all her trappings,
her nine little breasts bare, the
three little titties,
the three big boobs, and
the three leathery dugs,
and on one side of her
back the spinning wheel her
uncle had made her, and on
her left arm the leather
gauntlet for the bow over her
shoulder. tho some of her
arms were reaching out
others were pushing away, but
she had never seen fire
before, so she sat down.
it was also unclear to her
as to which was the bear.
soon this was discovered and
she turned into a reasonable

34 or 36, b or c cup. he
took one of her arrows, chopped
it in half, added a six-foot
long straight piece of locust
in the middle, and found himself
comforted able to stand up
holding this while she
slept. the bear kept growling
much of the time, as if to
say: hey bo, let's get
out of here.
                one day she
came upon agriculture.
the bear kept growling,
and every day the man laughed
with the bear, tousled its
hide, and turned back to
her. she still had all
those different arms, but
he thought there was a
key to that too, as to
the breasts. when the
crop of grain started coming
in he said to her: i
think i'll sit down and
invent whiskey. the bear
kept growling.
                    next, for
want of anything better to
do, they made a house.
he said, later, it was
to keep the bear out. he
figured he could stand
or sleep in the doorway,
holding the long arrow.

some say that that
first night in the house,
all her arms except two
disappeared, tho those

two kept all the
designs of the others.
in any event, she
said, now you're dealing
with reality. when
you invent whiskey, this
time, or peyotl, for i
forget which end of the
territory we're at, it'll
be religion, and good for you.

he put down the long
arrow and took her
to bed, where they lay
happily for a while, in
all conceivable positions.
then he invented writing.

SIRVENTES ON A SAD OCCURRENCE

it is spring; i can walk lightly
down the stairs even on the way
to work, and that's a gain—i
swing my hat widely, not cavalierly,
but remington, the old west, the three
mexican cowboys coming home off
the plains . . . the sun shines
even in my room, and my windows
are open, the pretty girls await
me in the street,
their coats open,
or no coats at all
                    and on her way
up the stairs an old lady loses
her control . . . i will write
against that which is in us to
make age an embarrassment in the
season of coming alive:
old lady, if at this point and
place in time, and all the world's
area, you cannot forget that small
muscle, if because of the fineness
of the day, your daughter, older than
my mother, says, momma, come, sit,
outside, all winter you've sat in,
the sun, the air, come momma, outside
you'll sit, and you go, painfully
the one flight down, and sit, and then
come up, and halfway up . . . don't
tell, mrs. stern, the daughter screams,
i'll be back, right away, i'll clean,
don't tell . . . what can she possibly
tell, old woman, that you are old,
that you have had your children, they
have had theirs, they, theirs, and
you are still here, your world

still exists, where does she fit in?
—as if there weren't already
shit in the the world, and you invented
it. what further indignities to
allow besides inventing shit?

and on top of it, as you clung to
the bannister at the top step, almost
around, fifteen feet from your
door, to face me suddenly, coming
down from one flight up, my hat no
longer swinging but over my head,
over my thin bearded face, my god
the moan then, even your daughter
scared by it, i thought you were
dying 'til i found out the truth:
me a tall skinny bearded eyeglassed
hollow-eyed ascetic jew, big
hat, you were back in poland—but
i am no rabbi, and it is no sin,
i am not the chasid or simple
ashkenazi reb you knew and
danced before, around, the psalms
went high to god, david i am
not, there's no cause for the
alarm, i'm so far removed from
it, all i could think was old
lady i wish i knew how to say
aspeto in yiddish, and couldn't.
old lady, it's spring, i love
you great grandma, this is a
natural act, why will you
fear me for it, i see each day
more shit than you could ever
dream of making, screw your
daughter, let mrs. stern watch
out for her own steps, i am just
standing here waiting for you
to pass, too late now for me
to go back up the stairs, i have

just discovered what the fact is
much too late, and will stand quietly.

and moving past it, later, after
you had been able to pass me,
to your door, me, going down the
steps, a warmth it offers
up, steaming like any simple load
of cow or horse shit, and the
clumsy kleenex streaks where your
daughter had started wiping, christ this
is the east side, let it sit there,
there is room for it, need for it,
labor does not create wealth, wealth
does not create wealth, shit creates
wealth, old lady, old lady, you are
the creator spirit, tho your tits
hang shrunken in your wrapper, tho
your man's long dead—i had a
woman once had need to pee each
time she came, the bed was
wet with it, but she had less need
old woman than you of simple
love that would allow such miscreant act.

this daughter then suckled like
we say at that long-dry breast too
long ago to give you back your due,
her pants were full too long ago to
let yours drop today.
let it go, old woman, let it go,
shit on it, let it go,
this is the east side, this
is park avenue, this is your
son the doctor riverside
drive yet, let it go, this
much you're entitled to, this
much even i can grant you, who
worries if he farts too loud
in his own silent room, who pisses
to the edge of the bowl it shouldn't

make no noise, who, like so many
of us, wakes each morning to either
constipation or the runs, this
much i can grant you, shit on
the stairs of my house, you
are old enough for that, remember
the little boys, they have not
yet learned how not to piss, they
stand at the curb, between two
cars, their feet spread and braced,
they arch over into the street
they fight each other, distance, the
pride, showoffs, why can't you
shit that easily on these
steps, old lady, i am sorry.

and it is spring, and where did
you think the flowers will come
from, the rain? and the pretty
girls if not from making love,
and the shit itself if not from
eating, and the broken noses and
the black eyes and scars if not
from fighting, this is the east
side, guns crack, people snort
their noses full of life, and you
are dying because you shat
upon these steps? and were faced
with me? old lady, act your age.

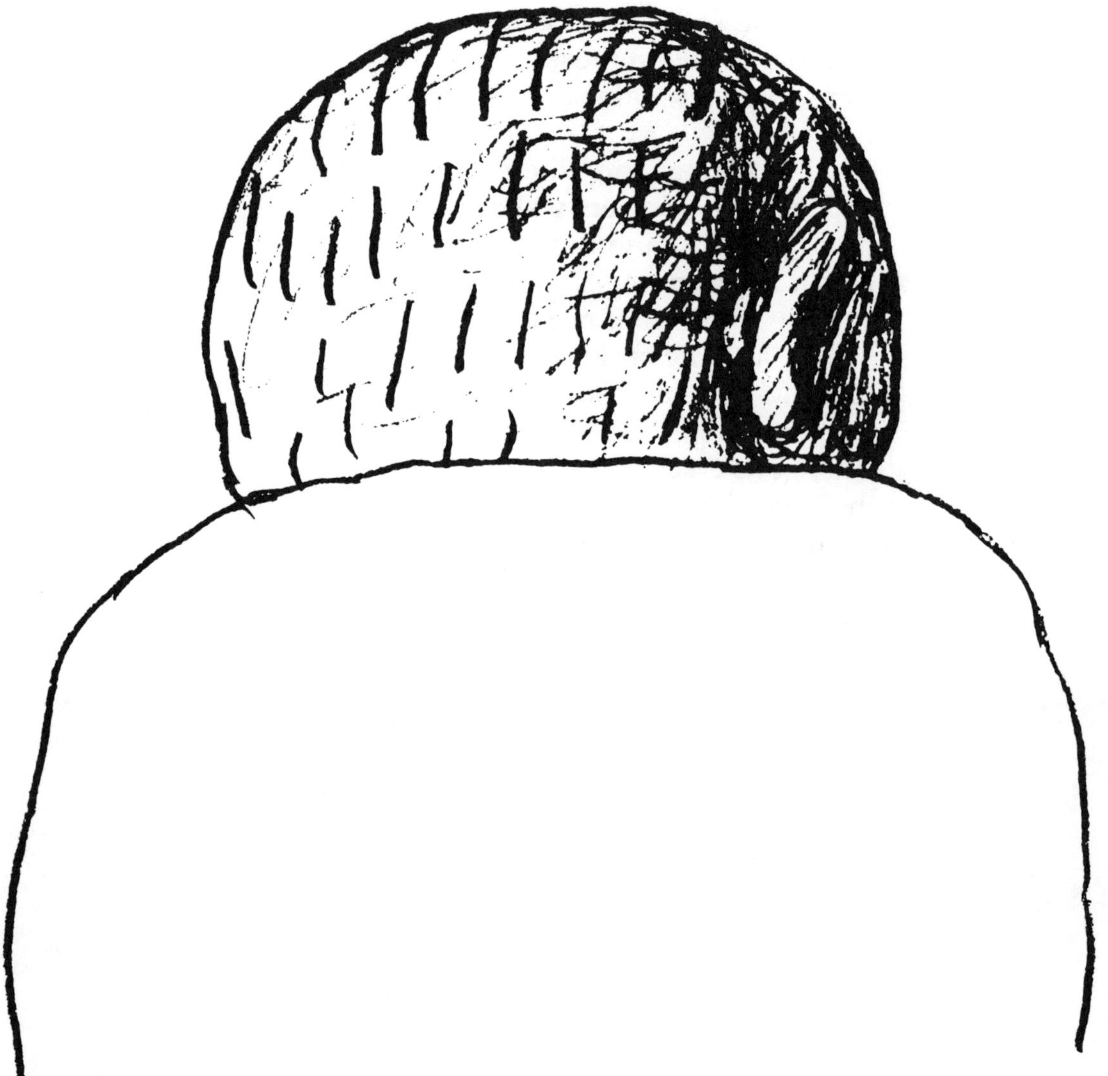

from **THE WRONG SEASON** (1973)

THREE BASEBALL POEMS

I

john g. "scissors"
mcilvain, described by
the sporting news as
remarkable, died
in charleroi, pa.,
recently. he was
88. he pitched for
22 minor league teams
in 15 different leagues
and was still in semi-
pro ball in his seventies.
when he won a 4–3 ball
game at seventy-five he
said: i don't see anything
to get excited about. i
think a person should feel
real good when he does
something unexpected.
i expected this. his
big disappointment was
that he never made the
majors, although he won
26 for chillicothe
one season, and 27 the
next. he was, however,
a bird-dog scout for
the indians for several
years. he had been
deaf since 1912.

II

andy the paperman at
bleecker and eleventh
is grungy, his paunch
and stubble offending
even me. he played
shortstop in the pennsylvania
league in 1941 and
believes "kids today
don't love the game
any more like we did."
he played against the
best of his time, major
leaguers and all, babe
dahlgren, sibby sisti,
you name 'em, he played
them all. he once
safely stole third through
a slough of mud, soaking
all through his shirt

III

on saturday, on
bleecker street a
shirt cardboard
hand-lettered in
the candystore window
:   spaldeens.

on sixth avenue, a
headline says
        society's laws
        force many u.s.
        citizens to live
        like caged animals

there's no sun, the
radio says rain. it
also says they're
playing. for real,
like shirt cardboard
signs. for real.

for real the rain came
sunday night. we were
one and one by then,
cleon three for seven,
i paced the kitchen
caged, an animal, the
rain kept coming down.

THINGS I CAN'T DO AT SHEA STADIUM

eat peanuts with no teeth;
drink beer, on the wagon;
order sandwiches, too goyishe;
stand the sodas, too sweet;
eat before i go, which means i have
to eat two hotdogs which aren't
very good; cheer a good player
on the other side if there's
any possibility of him hurting
us; pay absolute attention to
every play; open the out door
from the outside or the in door
from the inside in the johns,
nobody can; stand heights, i
think i'll fall into center
field; yell unselfconsciously
to "get a bingle" during a
rally, or start one off;
accept losing; accept winning.

from **ON OCCASION** (1973)

A GRACE

bless this house
and all who dwell
safe within its
living hell

OCCASIONS

FOR DAVID

eyes wide, we
have dumped it
in your lap. you
do not know that
yet. hands opened
and closed, the
panorama stretches
before you. you
do not know that
yet. lips ready,
you will take all
we have to give you.
and will survive.
and will pay us
back in our own
coin. even love,
if we come to deserve it.

A POEM FOR CHILDREN

the headline in the
poet's voice and intelligencer says
tom and paul have boys. we all
dance around the maypole, it
being that month and appropriate.
i have seen only little tom,
carlos t. awaits as he did for
nine months. i am assured
joanie looked beautiful two days
before term, a term they use. the
children will grow up my friends.

in itself a curious act, growing
up has been defined not once but
several times. not once did they
mention helicopters. not once did
they mention god being on the wrong
side, or the possibility of total
grace for a child who can't say the
word "park," no less "people's park."
they will grow up playing somehow and
finding their toys, even if the toys
are guns and the heads of their enemies:

>   for love, i would
>   split open, etc.

and if the toys destroy, who
asked for it? who taught it? my own
son smiled today to see me ask him
not to throw the ball—over went
the jug of water on the floor. i
yelled. he cried. i think that
he will live.
           what we are saying is
these children, born, are not going

to eat shit; i have a better hope for
it than ever—tom mcgrath is over
fifty! paul blackburn is over forty! joel
oppenheimer is over thirty! they are
breeding children! those children
will have children to learn from!
they will be immune from teargas!
they will come happily! even when
young! they will be able to like
tits without being hung up on them!
they will recognize cops in one-fifth
of a bartender's time! they will
even know how to play in parks! they
will even know how to shoot down
helicopters over the parks!

well, it's a dream, little tom,
carlos t., and nathaniel. i can't even
make you a school. i am trying.
someday maybe this world will be ready
for you, o knowledgeable of the earth.
someday maybe the world will say to
you where were you? we were waiting!
here is a sliding pond, slide down it;
here are swings, go swing on them.
i do not think so, but i will try
to give you some strength to do it,
all the while watching fervently the
skies, the helicopters, and the cops.

POEM

listen:
how many people listen when the hound howls?
when my uncle died and the people all were sad
they sat around his coffin and the hound sat
on top. for seven days
they sat darkened in the room with the hound howling
on top. clothes were ripped without pretense;
ties they'd never wear. they
sat around the coffin on hard benches and
they moaned and whispered and said they heard him
howl.
they let me walk in and see my uncle dead.
seeing them i felt i had to cry, to
say i saw the hound, but when i walked in
to see my uncle dead i heard a bark and i stopped
crying and i laughed instead because
my uncle once had shown me in december that
the way to warm your hands was to
blow through them clasped. we were happy then.

ANOTHER OLD MAN GONE

this one we'll miss, as he
gawks his way along, men-
acing. i wasn't allowed to
see him.
      with the police
sergeant arresting him,
he said: i can bring him
back to life. better a

conviction than a live man,
said the thirties—and yet
i always wanted to hear what
the old man would say about
the heart transplants. i
like to think it would be:
fellas, i was only acting.

i wish they hadn't scared
the shit out of me when i
was young. still, given
the strange age, people breaking
their ass, what else should
we have expected.

glomp glomp glomp he moves
in our dreams; he sits his
mother carefully before the
horrible machine, he says
hold still mother it won't
hurt you a bit. it didn't.
the fuzz were wrong! the
villagers were wrong! the
aristocrats were wrong!
boris karloff never hurt
nobody! boris karloff even
died carrying a cross out to
assuage the arabs!
                he was
an old man, eighty-one,
and he had his own heart.

FOR MATTHEW, DEAD

8 august 1967

at four, it seems to me, he
fell off the stump by the
mess hall, bruising the
hell out of his forehead
and nose, and a good deal
of screaming went on.

how shall we scream now,
when at twenty, he slipped
on a wet, moss-covered
ledge of north percy peak
and fell one hundred yards to
his death. at least this
made that decision for him:
he will neither serve in
lyndon's army, nor go to
jail, nor go to canada.
he was trying to scale the
peak by the west trail.

one half hour ago my own
son at eight months fell,
tripping in his walker.
it will not appear on the
book page of *the times*,
and we laughed instead of
screaming, to soothe him
down. this one has almost
eighteen years to make
his choice, and every day
a peril. good christ,
there are easier ways to
have decisions made. twenty
is no good time to die.

OBITUARY

paul de kruif you
are dead i read in
the times tuesday
march second, and
i am brought
back nine years
old reading my
brother's library *the
microbe hunters* how
i wanted to believe
it was all there,
koch over his
cultures, ehrlich
peering at
slides they were
going to make us
all healthy no more
diseases something went
wrong in our uni
verse but i wanted
then to believe and
did and dreamed of
all that could be
conquered a little
boy nine years old how
can i tell anyone what
you meant more than
albert payson ter
hune who after all just
talked of pets and
green fields and
loyalty, you talked of
killers and men who
saved us slaving in
laboratories oh
wernher von braun and

whoever invented
nerve gas when will
i read your obituaries
in *the new york times*
as the kids gather for
another workshop trying
to write a poem that
will save us from
diseases, despite
the obvious pun i
have my own koch
institute paul de
kruif and we are
hoping to find some
magic bullet, we
are hoping the answer is
as simple as finding
the problem with
the blood and how
to cure it, to cure
the ills of man.

FOR WILLIAM CARLOS WILLIAMS

i am angry because
there are still
birthdays
        and yet they
tell me you
are bad off. that
you are dying
           that
the last time you
went off they
thought you
were gone
        (at the
same time they
say you are
furiously
jealous—
          that someone
else can still
use a
right hand!

they tell me you
are an old man

they say when
you write new
verse they will not
take the
last one until
you write
the next
        they are
afraid you
will decide it
is all you

have to say.

it is
difficult to
talk about

:   how much land
you moved
into
      it is an old
story
no one is much
interested
            especially
in the face of it
that you are
still at
it.

the inheritance
will not be written
down and cannot be
contested

which is why there
is a need to
say something to
you. said straight
out without the
dignity of
image even—
            since if
you are dying then
you do not need
images now. rather
we should save
things to put
next to you which
you loved and
needed

that it should be
a good trip
        that you should
still be able to
move as it
was

(old man i
am living on
that land, developing
it, i.e., raising
houses and
cutting the timber

—like a dutiful
son the father
hates

—and it
makes me ashamed
sitting here
        no
matter how
busily

THE POLISH CAVALRY

for chas. olson, 1 january 1970

they stood there, in the mud,
one hundred thousand of them,
waiting for the panzers, and
they got it. there are certain
monoliths taught us something.
the estaurine ranges to thirty
feet, god knows how long he will
survive. what i am trying to say is
that you brought two generations
to life, and you'll have to
live with that. you always did move
like a grampus and you still do.
the polish cavalry at least had lances.
what you've got only your sons and
your grandsons know. the map of
the battle of the cowpens shows
what can be done with only a few
men, will you believe that now,
in your time of need? i'm sorry
i have to speak in different images,
but you told me a long time ago
to speak in my own, and i believed
that. you still are the man who
held a full pall mall like i
hold the stub of a gauloise, and though you
think you are prometheus, his liver
pecked at, for me you are odin.
let them take out an eye and give you
a gray cloak. you have saved us.

A PRAYER

> *for a wedding, 29 november 1963*

because everyone knows exactly what's good for another
because very few see
because a man and a woman may just possibly look at each
    other
because in the insanity of human relationships there still
    may come a time we say: yes, yes
because a man or a woman can do anything he or she
    pleases
because you can reach any point in your life saying: now i
    want this
because eventually it occurs we want each other, we want
    to know each other, even stupidly, even uglily
because there is at best a simple need in two people to try
    and reach some simple ground
because that simple ground is not so simple
because we are human beings gathered together whether
    we like it or not
because we are human beings reaching out to touch
because sometimes we grow
    we ask a blessing on this marriage
    we ask that some simplicity be allowed
    we ask their happiness
    we ask that this couple be known for what it is,
        and that the light shine upon it
    we ask a blessing for their marriage.

FOR JOHN AND LUCY

21 november 1970

aha! spring's a
long way off. the
bears shuffling into
caves. the world
slowing down, the
days gray. one
last fling 'til
sun comes back,
one more time
touching, feeling,
the wedding bells
will ring.
      the
bears find their
way slowly, they
do not choose quickly,
they spend the
year opting for
this berry, this
particular salmon.
ah, but when the
choice is made!
oh, most true of
all the zoo we are,
the bears.
      the caves
we sleep in are
the burnished thrones,
our ladies bedazzle
the universe.
      and
we nose our way
slowly, feeling the
year as few do,
picking the snow or

the spring or the
run of the fish or
the perfection
of the honey straight
out of air. go, let
the dance begin again,
let the cave glow
while the bear and
his lady sing, and
the world turns,
as we do, slowly,
and the spring
begins to build again,
endlessly. it will
greet you to wake
you soon, and
the world will
bless you, with
all its good things.
amen.

AN ANNIVERSARY

minnie and sam bukberg, 2 july 1967

for the newborn baby the
answer is simple: a large
stuffed gingerbread man. he
will sleep many nights with it.

and for the four year old
goddaughter, the answer is
also simple: a dress. she
is getting class to her now.

and for the newborn's mother,
though a little more
difficult, still, the
friends find a swinging robe,
just the thing to nurse in.

but what shall we do for
this couple, as we wander
though the stores? what can
we possibly buy that would make
sense. my wife is only half
as old as the time they have
lived together. how mount
fifty years simply on a
plaque? they have made their
children, they have their
grandchildren and their great,
and i, who am full of
words, can find none of
the proper ones. the ones
to say, as another did:
      they have fought, they have dug,
      they have bought an old rug . . .
but then, how else to mark it,
that in that time strength

flowed, and warmth. you
do not live fifty years with
another easily, yet it builds,
like the family, a pyramidal
structure, a strong base, the
point piercing heaven. and
the children find it so, home
base, and they walk the stores
fingering table linen, kitchen
ware, books, all the rest,
wondering what home base could
use—could use! after fifty
years!
     nathaniel, kiss your
great grandmother, and show
your smile while great
grandfather holds you in the sun.

BIRTHDAYS

   my grandmother was born in
'74, my father, '93.
i can grasp both dates.
they're both the same time.
she should be much older.
and your grandmother is
younger than my father.
that's what happens when
you marry a much younger woman.

FOR MY GRANDMOTHER

      12 august 1954

   the hot sun of
              summer reveals no woman as
                          nearly completely as you
reveal yourself, by your
            bearing, your face, your
                      actions; nor
seldom has.
        if it please you
                    you are my kind
of woman.

you know, as even
          others do, that we
                    all bear your stamp, and
i also, who
        am your grandson, youngest
                son of your

oldest son, i bear that
            stamp as much as any here
                        in this
company. but that stamp, again, is
            on our faces and
                        in the way we
hold ourselves.
            there is another.
                        not one of us
ever soured on life
            enough to say we made
                        a mistake.

you, too, at eighty
            continue as if you
                        were right.
it is good, in a
            bad time, and ensures
                        youth. no one
who married in ever
            understood this, and yet
                        it is as much a
part of our blood as, say, myself
            wearing my mother's
                        eyes, or that
my children
            will be light-haired.

                        you
are eighty, but i have
            to count on my fingers, to
                        figure the year of
your birth, and do not know
            anything other that
                        happened that year.

history does not
            concern me, or rather it
                        bores me, as it should
any live person.

                    so, may you
                              remember what it is
you will, either
          pleasant or no, as you
                    decide; i
who am your grandson
          salute you, and offer
                    myself. as in china
you would have my
          life to rule, here
                    i offer it for service, and
for now, this
          verse, words said in my
                    best voice; that
i may learn from
          you not how to
                    live, but
how to move—as you have
          moved, every day, alive in
                    the sun, as the
sun does, today,
          disclose, and in its good light
                    show you.

FOR A GODDAUGHTER

pretty miss jennifer
sweeter than any
flew through year one
and now it is done,
and two is coming
sweet as honey
          pat-a-cake, pat-a-cake, baker man
          giver her a kiss as fast as you can

A TRUNK

for eddie, 30 january 1971

as has been said too
often to bear re-
stating, but not
ever remembered: it
is not the generous
act so much as the
method of giving;
that, so many years
ago i tremble to
remember, he sat me
down in the polo
grounds, handed me
the pearl opera glasses,
and made me watch mel hein;
that i wore so many
suits of his, the whole
damned village thought
i had an italian tailor

name of cozzanetti; that
a trunk with his name
on it serves as my
linen closet now, our
sheets and pillowcases
and towels neatly
folded. the paint is
not bright, it was
painted 1938 i'd
guess to take him
off to college with,
but it sits in my
room, and the name
is there. it's
not a generous act
so much as the method
of giving, a gentle
concern.
      in this
he has never failed
no one, and we thank
him for it—but
i remember most the
hard benches, the man
yelling nest-lee, nest-
lee—the glamour of
learning it wasn't nestle's
i'd been eating—
the pants a little loose
about my waist, a
trunk.
      my linens, my
life, rest in it, thank
you.

SUE'S BIRTHDAY

dictated by nathaniel, age 3

what number does her live on
don't type the wrong number 'cause what number does she
      live on
what number
what number
(ssssh)
this one
right
so you won't forget, right

but sue's birthday couldn't be at nighttime
her going to have a cake
it going to be a big cake
it have to be a big cake

you know what my mom said
my mom said when the cake come i have a sip of her
      iced tea
a little sip
not all of it

when birthdays come then you say happy birthday

FOR FORTY

(a middle-distance race)

don't try more than
twice a night, with
lots of rest and
vitamins.
        eat
well. all
things in moderation.
greet the sun with
a smile, but don't
get bugged about rain.

exercise gently when
up to it. when
down to it, respect
it. love animals
and small children.
don't relate between
ages seven and twenty-four.

be a guru whenever
possible. bars are
good places, also
cocktail parties.

change your hat.
don't change your
underwear or socks.

read little if
at all, but believe
everything. give
answers whether you
know them or not.

grope every girl or woman

in sight, they expect
you to. cackle a lot.

don't sign anything.
stay away from high
insurance rates.
don't learn new tricks.
if you know something
forget it quickly.
write all phone
numbers down.

otherwise it's okay,
but avoid everything.
this too shall pass.

HAPPY NEW YEAR

i thought it would
be a different place, this
year at this time,

still the poem promised is
the poem to be delivered.

sing a different song then
from the one intended.

ah well if it hadn't been
the goyim, it would've
been somebody else, right?

next year, the promised land.

OTHERS

FOR C. B.

19 february 1971

who is clear, who
knows each poem, each
person, ought to
have a beginning, a
muddle, and a
end. she could
handle it, she said,
and i believed it.

THIS IS STOP TIME

in the marble cemetery
a tree is in bloom already

in the marble cemetery i can see
from my window, pink and white
blossoms of all things assault the
statuary, that's the only way to
look at it. pink and white the tree
stands in the middle of the marble cemetery.

marble itself often pink and white.
is this, then, why the pink and white
tree is blooming, there, in the middle . . .

and breakfast? i'm hungry.

the past that in us all does beat
will be our wine, will be our meat.

THE GIFT

with sureness she
irons her
cottons, the colored
and white take
shape. she works forcefully,
tests the heat of the
iron with the tip
of her finger wet
with her spit. skirts with
pleats, blouses both
simple and fancy, dresses.

the finished pile grows.

she knows summer is coming.

TIMESENSE

love an apple
seeds and core
we don't need to
know no more.

lovesong in *a flat*
hot or cold
never will
grow no more old.

vide: all that jazz.

THE AMERICAN SCHOOL

what we grind down to isn't dust or a fine edge.
what we grind down to no nub either.
i like the shape of your ass, and
the way your breasts hang.
when a woman has pulled us this far.
when a man has pulled us this far.
they know how to do it, well enough for anyone.

THE MIGRANT WORKERS

and if not god and
goddess, then—then
the old measure holds
true: fit enough at
least to pick blueberries
with you—and therein
lies the answer. the
patch lies before you, ripe
with berries, the two of you
picking like hell—why
not, why not
make a simple god-
damned pie, for once, for
once in your
life. put it on the
table legs sticking
up. a pie. a
simple berry pie.

BALSO'S BLUES

> *wrap me in your greasy arms, morph,*
slide me to sleep

in love's simplicity
it lies, in love's
simplicity we come to a
stark determination:
just what it's worth
losing sleep and hard-ons
working our asses off in
vain pursuit, trying
to pursue a trade! love
is a trade, why else settle
for clean shirts or an
evening's good meal. but,
if you won't understand this,
peace on your soul—which
i wanted to uncover, and whose
children i wanted to build slowly
or passionately in
the night and day.

did you imagine that man whose
most unofficial act is the
raising of his manhood would
ever consent to less a definition?
or able to make paradise
from bread and wine and you,
would find a trade denying it all?

the blues are what song sung.

WHAT THE

what the
addict said:
you
got to cold
turkey yourself,
man, nobody else
gone to do it.
or, believe and
you shall be saved,
saith the prophet.
this one, however,
is of neither per-
suasion this time of
year, rather slicing
his turkey cold, laying
the slices haphazard
and piled thick on
the bread into which
lovingly his yellow
blunted hollow teeth tear
yearningly swallowing
harshly and his dry
throat working to swallow
and remembering too late
there is cranberry relish,
with relish viewing
what the

UNTITLED

the man who wrote the
song probably never
knew the truth, but
love *is* a
many-splendored thing.

even the wan-ness moves
me but you won't
believe this, and
this sad ass shakes
itself to see you walk.

the belly is part
of it, your sweet
children move me,
a simple prick.

believe it, believe it.
the song sings for
spring as in other
seasons, only more so.

i beat with my
own sap rising, and
watch you from the
corners of my eyes.

i turn in bed toward
you and reach across
the void we need to
live in. i reach out
because i love you,
and loving you, can
rarely give, but mostly
take. thank god
you offer. it makes
a perfect match.

the man who writes
the song never knows
the truth. love is
a many-splendored thing.

FOUR PHOTOGRAPHS BY RICHARD KIRSTEL

A.
the party's over, but
only as billie sang
it, our hearts
breaking as her
voice did, our hearts
lifting like the
dolls are lifted, karen
picks up the dolls, they
are sprawled askew on
the floor, the flanks
of her body shine
before us, her breast
hangs, exposed, the
party's over, but
only as billie
sang it, so long ago,
our hearts breaking.

B.
sexual avarice! desire!
molly bloom saying yes,
i said yes, yes, yes, or
whatever that quote was . . .

karen is about to be
gone down on is the
point. down on! by
a doll! the doll is
going to eat karen! eat her
snatch! endanger that
pussy hidden in her fur!
she is not getting laid.
i am sorry for it! why
is she letting this happen?
why not a man? her tits
are lovely in this picture.

C.
mother, asleep in this picture
with your nipples erected, i
wish we could all rest so peaceably, i wish our lovers
would sleep next to us
with as little worry.

i wish all ribcages fell with
as clear a definition of life,
and that children could sleep
without suffering.
                      you lie there.
i am looking at you like a voyeur.
i am dreaming of what i will do
when you are awake, and then i won't
do it. it's the world we live in,
we can't eat our cake or have it
either. we turn restlessly
all night long, mother.

D.
the whore of babylon
has long legs.

THE SUM TOTAL

the estimates of my
age varied from nine to
almost dead. the little
girl said nine was a
teenager, teenagers
couldn't have children.
the other kid's older
brother said i must be
twenty-two; then
the discussion veered
to religion, mainly
who made babies. my
son soaked it all in,
learning in the gutter.
the catholic beat down
the pragmatist; she insisted
god in heaven made babies,
while he opted for
men and women. in the end, he
weakened, allowing as how
the mother and god made
the baby together, she
down here, he up in heaven.
the questioning began then:
your mother and father
married? my boy insisted
no! then they aren't your
father and mother she
told him. the other
boy's father had a sword and
three guns, he said—how
many your father got?
this was the only time my
son weakened, he turned to
me as i sat on the bench in
the sun, looking the question
at me. none of them saw
my one finger raised to

him in answer. one, he
said. the other boy backed
off. then the little
catholic girl said that
god was in heaven. up
there, the older boy said.
he pointed. that cloud isn't
heaven, my boy said. no,
said the little catholic girl,
that cloud is air—but
do you know who the first
president was? of america?
yes. richard nixon. no,
she screamed, it was
george washington, and
lincoln was . . . as she
paused i prayed she'd
be wrong. the sixteenth!
i'm four and a half,
my son said, in the
march sunlight, 1971.

THE KOPF THAT CHEERS

the comforting sound of
the water filling the tub,
the bite of the grapefruit
juice, no, not morning, it's
night, the day's work is
done, the beer and stout
stand on the table and
the glass of them, mixed,
has that guinness face on
it i remember from before the
war—that face and the
dubonnet man—in any
event, night, and the
juice just to clear my
throat, tho it clear my
head too. i remembered the
first time, it was because in
the midst of talking, you
saying no, maybe, no, i,
a little high, said:
when shall i pick you up.
it's enough excuse for a song.

COME ON BABY

walking out on the street saturday
noon—history which
piles up had not prepared
me, not at all—as in
the worried eyes of the guy
running numbers who had once
worked a proof press with me

a fear grew of where did
he know me from and could
only, stutteringly, ask
did i live here? yes, i answered.

or the fact that the tie
i wanted still lay tangled
in my dark green shirt at
the bottom of the heap on
the chair, and it was that
shirt, too, that i had also
wondered about, not in the clean
shirts, not in the dirty, and
not mine, either, come to
think of it, larry's which
he left here one day when we
thought the world was waiting
for us, and so took a clean
one of mine. or what is a good
jewish boy doing reading chester
himes and drinking dant on shabbas?

history you who pile up you have
not prepared me for any fact of
my life. who knows what shadows
lurk in the hearts of old girl
friends, for example, that she
should be bugged at my own
admissions finally made of
the hopelessnesses. she could
have laughed it away i suppose
instead of getting hurt—as if
i had slashed her with words, look
out of someone else's eyes her
girl friend said—goddamn it i'm
only human, got two eyes, myopic
and astigmatic, corrected to damn-
near perfect with glasses, whose
eyes should i look out of?

AT ELEVEN-FIFTEEN

i wonder what that
tune was, eight years
ago. we dancing, me
bombed, and the surge
of love so big i
crashed backward
into the wall,
later got violently
sick on the floor.

meanwhile, in 1941,
we danced awkwardly
with louises and
lillians, the wind-up
phonograph, the cactus
needles, bing crosby,
buddy clark, and, then,
sinatra. the girls
giggling as they led
us round the floor.

at night the remotes
came in, nat brandywine
from the roof of
kansas city's best
hotel, or harry kool
from glen island casino.
this poem can never be
finished correctly.

THE ONLY ANARCHIST GENERAL

the architecture fell into
place only at night, the paths
led somewhere, the lights
lit them, even the low
wall had a reason finally,
it comforted me walking.

my wife questioned my
orders as if i weren't a
general. the bridge still
frightens me, *not* the ravine,
which is why it is necessary
to make friends with trolls,
constantly. still, i met my people
halfway home, and walked back in company.

my wife questions my orders as if i
were not the only self-taught happy
genius of my household. i note
crests and rises, point out
defensible positions. the
armies move and swell, the
battle is coming. my wife
questions my orders. i am an
anarchist general shouting orders in a
strictly formed landscape. my children
did leave me here knocking on wood,
i walk the bridge alone in the night's
landscape, thinking of low
walls, covering the terrain.

THE LADIES OF WESTBETH

I
because you were seventeen when
we met, i was older then. fourteen
years difference is fourteen years
difference, but seventeen is a
special age for women, and your
pale flesh sent me leching across
long island, holding your hand on
beaches, straining my eyes when the
bikini shifted. you were young then,
i've always been one who lusted for
pretty young goyim, the thin
blondes turning tan in the summer sun.

then you turned twenty-eight and
i went past forty. i talk to you
now by the elevator, discussing our
various interests; i even tried touting
you onto our cat, to take her along
with your two, getting her out of my
marriage bed. because i'm happier
with my lady, no doubt of it, and
the leching is gone—but still it would
have been nice, baby, if you'd seen
more than the dirty old man, if you'd
taken your bathing suit off, balled
me, even answered my call, or thanked
me for sending the poems.
                              instead you
brought me your own poems ten years
later, no longer a pretty blonde goy
teasing the horny poet with sweetness,
sweetness of seventeen-year-old flesh
tanning away in the summer sun. why
should i care about your mind, lady?

II
your daughter now lounges around
this building turning all of us on.
one day she said that i knew you,
she said that i used to run with
her mother. so i found out
that you had a kid when i sat
as a junior member of the board.
frankly, i didn't want to come on, then,
but the thought would occur, late
at night. everybody else in the
bar was making out, why shouldn't
i? that's how it was in the good
old days. now i don't want any
either, but like to tease your
daughter because young women
are pleasures in any event.

III
you were eleven, your sister nine or
ten; i was an early twenty. old
as i thought i was i was still
a kid. the difference was that
you knew your own age. now your
son plays with mine, your husband
and i talk about the meaning of
habnab and somewhere twenty years
have gone up the flue, under the
bridge, disappeared. if you watch
the kids this afternoon, i'll
take them tomorrow morning.

IV
your ex-husband maligns me in
his books, turns my first
wife into what he wanted you to
be; you walk in the yard with
strange men and big dogs. your
son can talk to me, your daughter
has the biggest tits in the building.

i used to think about yours, while
my first marriage was breaking apart.

V
you were standing on
the corner and i
passed by at first
not recognizing you.
after all it was
ten years ago. like
we say we aint gettin
any younger. in the
morning, with the
coffee cooking i put
my arms around you.
why are you romantic
in the morning you
said. i couldn't
quite believe it.

which makes me think
it was just as well
altho that is a
bitterness we're not
allowed to have. i
would have felt much
better if i had known
that quiet line right off
passing by the corner.
why *am* i romantic
in the morning?

THE NEWS

she'd been sick three
weeks, couldn't cook, couldn't
stand the raw food, her
stomach settling down only when
finally supper got a little
food in her
          when the doctor
called, the diagnosis confirmed,
motherhood again, she
ate all my strawberry cheese
napoleon, then told me.

PEOPLE ARE STARVING IN EUROPE

why are they always bringing
me food? italian hors d'oeurves,
french cookies. what i am
asking is something else, their
own sweet bodies, or in the
one case just keep the hell
out of here. yet the food
piles in. yet if there was
love and you were hungry how
carefully tread asking for a
meal—and buy the food.

but i would still like to know
just what the french cookies
indicated, if not a turn-off
from that particular woman i
wanted to eat, not even like
a gourmet, but, rather, hungrily.

to say, even, i missed it.
but this is not so good to
hear, she would prefer, i
suppose a statement more like
this: i didn't care, i had
other rows to hoe, other
cunts to plow. as she being
woman had her hoes to row,
and plows to cunt.
                      my sickness
is i want to fuck my love and
love my fuck. as i want
to turn my luck into a pack
of tarot, waiting to be
laid out and read. as i want
to find this world a sensible
place. as i want to know
why the french cookies, why
italian hor d'oeuvres, why
rum napoleons, and none of
you brought your cunt along,
or draped it with balls i
didn't wish to be concerned
with. or that vain hope i
keep having that while you
are cooking i'd be buying the
sweet french cookies for the
dessert we would serve while
waiting for the guests to get
the fuck out of there, so we
could concern ourselves with
more relevant matters, rather
than with whether the coffee
is done, and who wants cream
and sugar. you bring yours
and i'll bring mine, and i'll
be in scotland when you are.
then we'll have dinner.

THE ALL-STAR

the weight of the petals
makes them fall
one two three four
the first was
outside, the next two, low

the last crossed the plate
a little inside

"that would have been nice
that would have been something at time like this
i wish i had, to tell you the truth
but maybe it's better i didn't swing
i might have been embarrassed
i might have popped it up."

THE ACT

as i do
it is as it is
does as it does
as i am it is
is as is is as
i do as i do
as it does as it
does as it is
as is is

ZEN YOU

as we were involved in this
dart game where nobody seemed
able to hit the bull's-eye which
was necessary to end it, i
turned to my partner and said if
i use zen, that is to say, if i
worry only about the dart and
allow the dart the problem of
the target, perhaps?

                good
christ no! he shouted—worry about
the fucking bull's eye and let the
dart take care of itself, for
christ's sake.

           i took aim, carefully.
the dart flew straight to the bull's-eye.
oh well, this is the west, we
do things differently, i suppose.

THE ILIAD

in a somewhat condensed transliteration for modern readers

helen had a snatch
all filled with honey;
paris had a ball
was made of money.
they went off to
ball and joy—
that was the start
of the fall of troy.
(she was stolen away
from the king of greece—
it caused more fussing
that the golden fleece.)
agamemnon called
his boys all in,
said, yessir boys,
got to stop their sin.
all the gang
from near and far,
including lads
without one scar,
jumped in the boats
and started to paddle;
hector started oiling
his boots and saddle.
most got hurt,
a lot were dead,
but helen ended
back in aggy's bed.

this proves a moral
often told:
ain't nothing finer
than a custom rolled,

but of all the
most unkindly cut
is got for smoking
another's butt.

VERITIES

george, in this
life one can't be
right all the
damned time. i
hate those corn
muffins i bought
for breakfast. they
did not taste good
to me. they did
not taste good to
me. damn it, they
did not taste good
to me at all.

THE BODY POLITIC

halfway between
night and morning.
middle night.
soft haunch of
thigh. cushion,
as noted before,
derived from
the word for
thigh. persian?
i don't know, know
only the ease of
soft haunch of
thigh, middle
night. halfway
between young and
old, mid-age. too

old to do, too
young not to
want to do. the
poisons erupting
through the flesh,
the body politic
revolting, casting
its poisons, boils,
carbuncles, all
manner of fevers.

halfway between
pity and rage all
at one's self, cursed
for what's not
done, cursed for
what is to do.

the white meat of
tender haunch mixes
with gigot roti,
properly pink and
tender, next to
white beans, and
one avoids other
images of meat. this
is enough to stop
sex and eating, crossing
each other. leave
the rest of the
acts for yourself.
they are little enough.

if i could i would
drink this all out.
that doesn't work
just now, not even
watching the wine
being poured, just
as the blue lines
carry the blood

beneath the
flesh of the
thigh. i promised
not to speak of
blood spurting,
but what of the
juices of the
gigot, in the
plate, next to the
white beans? what
of the middle
night? what of the
pull in two directions?

which way with the
body politic turning
each way, rotting
a little each
time the decision
is made, what about
the body politic i
promised also not
to speak of, the sins
responsible for
committed or not?

i am too old, or
i am too young, and
the body does not
know what to do,
which choice to make.
the body's confused.

god help us, maybe
the first choice
was right, it is
the soft thighs
will save us, if
we can get past the
other images of flesh,
if we can forget

what we do to
blood, if we, for
god's sake, stop
doing it, and
once again turn
human, in middle
night, in mid-age,
in all the turnings
of the body and
the head, in all
our twisted reasoning.

AMERIKA, THE BEAUTIFUL

       *   Oh, beautiful for specious lies
   *   *
*   *   for somber yields of grain
   *   *   for poison-tainted travesty.
    *   above the blighted plain.
Amerika, Amerika, god's turned his face from thee
and crowned thy greed with stunted seed
from tree to dying tree.

SOME CHILDREN, KANSAS, ONE NIGHT, OTHER THINGS, ANOMALIES

on the night when what was left of the
good things came to an end, i called
new mexico. i am always calling somewhere,
but birthdays are different. the older
one answered, and i found at thirty-eight
i had a son with a bass voice. kansas
was voting and so was nebraska.
                                 i can't
even get angry anymore, i'm tired,
they have taken the country away. who
cares? who can care anymore? even
karl shapiro is writing "frankly
erotic" poetry!
                now american flags will
fly everywhere. what happened? they
never saw a black man, and they believe
that the air they breathe is pure.

meanwhile, the simple fact is that strom
delivered and mayor daley didn't. i
hope it is remembered. what could i
tell that boy with the bass voice, or
his brother who had just turned thirteen,
or, even, the new one here, two, running
nose, not only not knowing why i had
brushed him off my lap to follow the
night, but not even knowing yet how to
blow his own goddamned nose, offering
it up to me, dripping, over and over to be wiped.

what shall we do? what shall we do? shave?
settle down? shut up? pack the bags?
will there still be passports? o my people,
my poor dear father convinced that i'm
wrong, anthony imperiale convinced he is
right, spiro t. agnew convinced he's vice-
president and deserves to be . . .
                               and
why not marry the richest man in the world?
why not? why not be a sixty-two year old in
queens celebrating by firing your rifle with
the arms cache inside the house—and why
not give up the dream, move out, take
your children with you, go? why not?

in "one of the most closely fought
elections in american history" who
really gives a damn, save the worst?

gentlemen, i give you the president
of these united kansas.

NAPALM POEM

tomorrow is groundhog day.
when i poke my head out of the burrow
what will i see?

sons off to the west,
and one i neglect here at home.

women i have balled
not to their own satisfaction.

women, countless, i have turned
onto numerous perversions.

students i have not taught.

bosses i have given no work, and

friends i take money from.

i do not think any of these
have burned scars ribbing their bodies.
i do not think any of these
says oppenheimer go home.
i do not think they writhe
cursing my sins.

perhaps i am wrong
let them come forth.
let them arraign me. let them
curse me with bad dreams.
let the heavens open up and rain
down on me, my sins, those i have hurt.
let my sleep be bad. let my
appetites disappear. not one of them
has died or lived crippled because of me,
even tho i be a dirty-minded poet. they
have grown, somehow. they live, somehow.

i know you will not listen, you
have made up your minds. it
burns me up the way they carry on, you say.
i know this. i ask you to think just once
of what you are doing. fuck up a woman for love,
that is a better crime. fuck up a
child for love. that is a better crime.

        napalm, napalm, burning bright
        in the jungles and the night
        what immoral hand or eye
        framed that searing body's cry?

MORATORIUM

wednesday, 15 october 1969

the little boy wasn't three yet,
and as the crowd grew, carrying
candles, it was hard to know what
he thought about it. he, himself,
wasn't carrying a candle but had
a large corrugated cardboard whale,
it had giant teeth, and he held it
high and proud. four people looked
at it and said noah the whale, and
one oohed moby dick, but most didn't
say a thing. it was a silent march.
the little boy got tired, but he would
keep walking, so he gave the whale to
his father. now it rode high above
the crowd; people were asking what
is it? and, why carry a whale in
a peace march?
                i tried to answer
that they were dying more quickly than
us, so it seemed to make sense. some
looked at the two of us very strangely,
a few heard what we were saying.
                                    they
are killing the whales so fast that
the fleets come back half-full ahead
of time—and a male blue whale can
swim his whole life without ever
finding a mate. this should tell us
what sort of a beast we are, how we've
learned to draw leviathan forth from
the sea, and kill him. from the
beginning we knew how to kill ourselves.

POEM WRITTEN IN AND FOR NEW YORK CITY

the blue whale and the
sperm whale are dying.
only the children
can tell us this.

the wolf is an
"endangered species,"
spending his life with
the stronger bowing
to the weaker in any
internecine battle.
only the children can
tell us this.

the air is dying, every
breath catching harder.
only the children can
tell us this.
    the water
at the beaches may or
may not be fit to swim
in this summer, they say.
only the children can
tell us this.
    the noise
pounds on the head, which
leads to madness. this is
provable, but only the
children can tell us this.

people are dying from hunger.
only the children can tell
us this.
    people are dying from
napalm. only the children
can tell us this.
     people are
dying from bullets and bombs.

only the children can tell
us this.

       children are dying,
killed by other children, or
by men hired for the public
safety, and again and again
and again only the children
can tell us this.

          thank god
they do. thank god they
have learned how stupid we are.

but i am proud of the
children, and i grieve
that they die while we
live, and that we have
to depend on the
children to tell us.

no child ever dug an oil well,
but many have tried to
get through the core of
the earth to get to china
as any child will tell you.

AS WE GO MARCHING ON

the last time was
1932. they were
asking for bread.

mr. macarthur wore an
english-tailored
uniform with hand-
embroidered insignia,
and set the american
records for rows of
ribbons with seven.
he sat on a horse.
the veterans in the
bonus army, they
threw stones and he
did not once flinch.
this was reported in
his obituary in *the
times*. there were
also some machine guns
and some tanks around
him. douglas macarthur
was an american hero.
no one ever had to
tell him his duty.

one hundred members
of the eighty-second
airborne said they
would throw down their
arms and join the
demonstration if ordered
to fire.

      how many rows
their medals make? how
many purple hearts to
weigh down your blouse,
general? out front,

how many hands never no
more to stitch in
silver and gold the
insignia of a general in
the united states army?
how many legs not to
wear high polished
boots? how many men
growing saigon bluegrass
to feed your horse to
put your rump on? what
do you die for, general?

AUTHOR'S NOTE

"selecting the poems for this edition has given me the opportunity to correct some typos, as well as change a very few lines where the syntax has been getting in my way for years. essentially, these poems are, as i believe they should be, as they were written however long ago. of course i would write some of them differently today, and some maybe not at all, but isn't that the point? or, the only thing that does not change, etc.

"and i would be guilty of enormous ingratitude if i did not thank robert bertholf, george butterick, david landrey, don melander, and terry smith, who expended time and energy helping me select the poems; and jonathan williams, publisher, and tom meyer, the jargon amanuensis, who are, god bless them, still at it; and, of course, the beautiful theresa maier, who made sure i kept at the scut work necessary to get the manuscript done, and took the worst of it to do herself."

AN INDEX TO TITLES AND FIRST LINES

TITLES OF POEMS ARE SET IN BOLD FACE

17–18 APRIL, 1961, *149*
A, *20*
a bosom of, *30*
A FABLE, *163*
A FIVE ACT PLAY, *80*
A GRACE, *207*
A GRACE FOR PAINTERS, *51*
A HEART FULL OF, *27*
A LONG WAY, *112*
A LOVE POEM, *82*
A MAGAZINE, *183*
a man was out walking his, *189*
A NOTE, *98*
A POEM FOR CHILDREN, *212*
A POEM IN TUNE WITH ITS TIME, *68*
A POSTCARD, *26*
A PRAYER, *92, 223*
a quieter man could not, *39*
a tenacious man, *115*
A TREATISE, *131*
A TRUCK, *231*
A VALENTINE, *100*
according to the latest, *142*
AFRICAN MEMORIES, *178*
aha! spring's a, *224*
AMERIKA, THE BEAUTIFUL, *269*
AN ANNIVERSARY, *226*
AN ANSWER, *9*
AN APPROACH TO LE BAIN, *16*
AN UNDEFINED TENDERNESS, *37*
and if not and, *243*
and that sweet, *102*
andrew jackson, now my, *170*
andy the paperman at, *200*

ANOTHER OLD MAN GONE, *214*
anything else would be frivolous, *68*
APOCRYPHA, *39*
APRIL FOOL, *35*
AQUARIUS, *140*
as has been said too, *231*
as i do, *261*
as if i were going to make, *29*
as if it weren't what we had, *119*
AS WE GO MARCHING ON, *276*
as we were involved in this, *262*
AT ELEVEN-FIFTEEN, *254*
at four, it seems to me, he, *216*
BALSO'S BLUES, *244*
because everyone knows exactly what's good for another, *223*
because you were seventeen when, *256*
birds sing and my, *35*
BIRTHDAYS, *228*
bless this house, *207*
BLONDE LADIES' SONNET, *108*
BLOOD, *35*
blood red the rust from, *72*
BLUE FUNK, *25*
BRONXUS, *174*
but i thought i, *81*
CARTOGRAPHY, *31*
CLAMS ON THE HALF SHELL, *79*
COME ON BABY, *252*
DEAR MISS MONROE, *165*
don't try more than, *234*
DREAMS OF GLORY, *158*
eat peanuts with no teeth, *202*
EDUCATION: THE MUSEUM OF OUR YOUTH, *176*
ends, *65*
every sunday nite it's, *121*
every time, *9*
everyone else is writing you, why, *165*

eyes wide, we, *211*
first she comes down it ta dum ta dum ta, *13*
FLORA, *83*
FOR A GODDAUGHTER, *231*
FOR C.B., *241*
FOR DAVID, *211*
FOR FORTY, *234*
FOR JOHN AND LUCY, *224*
FOR MATTHEW, DEAD, *216*
for my grandmother, *228*
FOR THE BARBERS, *33*
for the newborn baby the, *226*
FOR WILLIAM CARLOS WILLIAMS, *219*
FORMAL VERSE, FATHER OF SEVENTY-THREE, *28*
FOUND ART, *98*
FOUR PHOTOGRAPHS BY RICHARD KIRSTEL, *248*
fourth day. work, *108*
friends, *131*
from the heart of a flower, *38*
geometry's my, *25*
george, in this, *265*
giving what you have on, *174*
half-bent and crouched holding, *37*
halfway between, *265*
hang them up on the wall, the, *176*
HAPPY NEW YEAR, *236*
he dreamt of himself, *138*
he will insist on, *12*
helen had a snatch, *263*
How, ever else to, *35*
i am angry because, *219*
i am concerned with impossibilities, the, *84*
i believe you, i, *123*
i fuck you, *172*
i have few clothes and, *97*
i know your door, *78*
i suck at your, *105*

283

i thought it would, *236*
i wish all the, *25*
i wonder what that, *254*
if i don't bring you, *17*
if it were only, *104*
if what one were about was, *98*
images of J____ assail him, *10*
in february the, *140*
in love's simplicity, *244*
in new england, *112*
IN THE BEGINNING, *97*
in the gray mist that, *163*
in the marble cemetery, *241*
in the neck he, *32*
in the touch—if, *98*
in time, in time they, *13*
it is spring, *192*
it seemed to me when i saw her, *41*
ivory box, you, *110*
john g. "scissors", *199*
KEEPING IT, *108*
LA REVOLUCION, *72*
last night, put to it, shaking, *111*
LEAVE IT TO ME BLUES, *39*
LESSON I, *59*
LET ME GO HOME WHISKEY, *107*
let's put it this, *26*
liberty to be defended on, *156*
LIFE AS IT IS LIVED, *170*
like a flower grows, i, *82*
like the baroness, a, *79*
likely the lions swing, *139*
listen, *214*
love an apple, *242*
love ends neither cleanly nor dirtily, *118*
love is not memory, love, *77*
LOVESONG, *13*
MARE NOSTRUM, *30*
MATHEMATICS, *186*

MAY DAY IN THE PARK, *21*
MID-PASSAGE, *29*
MODERN TIMES, *106*
money is paper i, *53*
MORATORIUM, *273*
MY BLUE HEAVEN, *36*
my grandmother was born in, *228*
N. B., *77*
NAPALM POEM, *271*
never seen cars race, *68*
NEW BLUES FOR THE MOON, *78*
no zoos anywhere in, *170*
now you are dead, *180*
O Jung, O Adler, O Freudian, shrinker of heads, *180*
OBITUARY, *217*
Oh, beautiful for specious lies, *269*
oh, the word, and the, *92*
OKAY, *53*
olaf the, 121
OLD STORY, *189*
ON PARADE, *32*
on saturday, on, *201*
on the left branch, a, *19*
on the night when what was left of the, *269*
one more kind act the, *80*
ORPHEUS, *47*
our rightful place, *158*
pablo neruda was one, so, *55*
PASSING THE TIME AWAY, *172*
paul de kruif you, *217*
PEIRE VIDAL AT THIRTY-TWO, *81*
PEOPLE ARE STARVING IN EUROPE, *259*
people around here all, *174*
POEM, *158, 214*
POEM FOR LOUD LAUGHTER, *65*
POEM FOR NEW CHILDREN, *70*
POEM IN DEFENSE OF CHILDREN, *156*
POEM IN PRAISE OF PERSEVERANCE, *105*
POEM ON THE DEATH OF WCW 3/4/63, *180*

285

POEM WRITTEN IN AND FOR NEW YORK CITY, *274*
PREFACE, *25*
pretty miss jennifer, *231*
PROVENCE, *14*
PUBLIC AFFAIRS, *156*
QUADRIVIA, *70*
riding my own, having, *117*
rose tits jam made of, *142*
Runs, *59*
SEIZE THE DAY, *148*
seized by, *172*
she sits, *11*
she'd been sick three, *259*
SIRVENTES ON A SAD OCCURRENCE, *192*
SIX-DAY AND BALL-BEARING, *117*
SOME CHILDREN, KANSAS, ONE NIGHT, OTHER THINGS, ANOMALIES, *269*
sometimes the culture, *183*
STUDIES IN ARABIA DESERTA, *174*
SUE'S BIRTHDAY, *233*
SUNDAY MORNING, *115*
SWEET BLUES AND OTHER SONGS, *102*
tenderly as a, *33*
THE 150th ANNIVERSARY OF THE BATTLE OF NEW ORLEANS, *170*
THE ACES, *68*
THE ACT, *261*
THE ALL-STAR, *261*
THE AMERICAN SCHOOL, *243*
the anchorage for explosives is in his heart, *30*
THE ANSWER, *17*
THE ANYBODY BLUES, *29*
the architecture fell into, *255*
THE BATH, *12*
the blue whale and the, *274*
THE BODY POLITIC, *265*
THE BOYS WHOSE FATHERS, *55*
THE BREADWINNER, *39*

THE BRUSHES, *115*
THE BUS TRIP, *10*
the ceiling of his bedroom, *31*
THE CHART, *30*
THE CLASH, *110*
the colors we depend on are, *40*
the comforting sound of, *252*
THE COUPLE, *17*
THE DANCER, *5*
THE ECONOMY OF ART, *121*
the estimates of my, *250*
the eye, the, *20*
THE FAKE SMILE, *180*
THE FEEDING, *21*
THE FOURTH ARK ROYAL, *60*
THE GARDENER, *19*
THE GIFT, *242*
THE GOD, *12*
the headline in the, *212*
THE HEART, *138*
the hot sun of, *228*
the idea of, *115*
THE ILIAD, *263*
the incredible delicacy, *16*
the innocence of her, *145*
THE INNOCENT BREASTS, *145*
the kings march and the, *158*
THE KOPF THAT CHEERS, *252*
THE LADIES OF WESTBETH, *256*
the last time was, *276*
THE LESSON, *172*
the little boy wasn't three yet, *273*
THE LOVE BIT, *40*
THE LOVER, *9*
THE LOVING MACHINE, *142*
the man who wrote the, *246*
THE MIGRANT WORKERS, *243*
THE MIND IS THE EASY WAY OUT, *104*
THE NEW NIGHTGOWN, *123*

287

THE NEW STANDARD SIMPLIFIED CABALA FOR HOME USE, *110*
THE NEWS, *259*
the Old Woman sits at, *148*
THE ONLY ANARCHIST GENERAL, *255*
the party's over, but, *248*
THE PEACHES, *19*
THE POEM, *100*
THE POLISH CAVALRY, *222*
THE PRESENT, *163*
THE RIDDLE, *162*
the ring of it then, *163*
THE SCENE, *37*
the shape of the heart, *100*
THE SLIDING POND SONNET, *13*
THE SUM TOTAL, *250*
THE SURGEON IN SPITE OF HIMSELF, *111*
THE THREE AND A HALF MINUTE MILE, *118*
THE THREE OLD LADIES, *120*
THE TIDE, *11*
TRE TORN NIGHTGOWN, *41*
THE TRAVELLERS, *144*
the weight of the petals, *261*
the word peace, *21*
THE YOUNG BLOODS, *40*
there are waterfalls pour, *70*
therefore to open, *47*
they are fighting, she, *178*
they have returned, *100*
they stood there, in the mud, *222*
THINGS I CAN'T DO AT SHEA STADIUM, *202*
this is, *17*
THIS IS STOP TIME, *241*
this morning plum, *114*
this one we'll miss, as he, *214*
tho it, *36*
THREE BASEBALL POEMS, *199*
thus, *34*
time is an old lady, *60*
TIMESENSE, *242*
today i bathed my feet, like, *14*

tomorrow is groundhog day, *271*
TRIPLETS, *34*
UNTITLED, *246*
VERITIES, *265*
walking out on the street saturday, *252*
wandering jew even, *83*
we come to another place, *186*
well at last i am done with it, *149*
well he cries out behind bars, *29*
well, i will break myself once more against, *108*
what i worry about is you and what, *28*
what is it in me won't, *120*
what mercy is not, *9*
what number does her live on, *233*
WHAT THE, *245*
what we dream of in our easiest, *39*
what we grind down to isn't dust or a fine edge, *243*
what will happen to your, *40*
what's all the shouting about, the, *156*
what's gray and comes in quarts, *162*
when drunkenly i groped you first, *107*
when i was fifteen i read spenser, *110*
when she fed the, *21*
WHEN THE DRUMS STOPPED, *138*
WHEN WHAT YOU DREAM, *84*
when your belly, *19*
where, *12*
where you are there are chairs, some, *51*
who is clear, who, *241*
why are they always bringing, *258*
wind rattles windows, *106*
with sureness she, *242*
world, before us like a, *70*
WRONG AGAIN, *14*
YESTERDAY, *114*
you where you are, ensconced, *144*
ZEN YOU, *262*
ZEUS IN MAY REFLECTS ON A RECENT LETTER   289
  FROM ASTARTE, *119*
ZOO STORY, *121*